Instructor's Manual
and Test Bank
to Accompany

GROUNDWORK FOR COLLEGE READING

Fourth Edition

GROUNDWORK FOR COLLEGE READING

WITH PHONICS

Fourth Edition

TP

Books in the Townsend Press Reading Series:

Groundwork for College Reading
Groundwork for College Reading with Phonics
Ten Steps to Building College Reading Skills
Ten Steps to Improving College Reading Skills
Ten Steps to Advancing College Reading Skills
Ten Steps to Advanced Reading

Books in the Townsend Press Vocabulary Series:

Vocabulary Basics
Groundwork for a Better Vocabulary
Building Vocabulary Skills
Building Vocabulary Skills, Short Version
Improving Vocabulary Skills
Improving Vocabulary Skills, Short Version
Advancing Vocabulary Skills
Advancing Vocabulary Skills, Short Version
Advanced Word Power

Other Reading and Writing Books:

Everyday Heroes
English Essentials
English at Hand
Voices and Values: A Reader for Writers

Supplements Available for Most Books:

Instructor's Edition
Instructor's Manual and Test Bank
Online Exercises

Copyright © 2008 by Townsend Press, Inc.
Printed in the United States of America
9 8 7 6 5 4 3 2 1

ISBN-13: 978-1-59194-097-5
ISBN-10: 1-59194-097-4

**For book orders and requests for desk copies or supplements,
contact us in any of the following ways:**

By telephone: 1-800-772-6410

By fax: 1-800-225-8894

By e-mail: cs@townsendpress.com

Through our website: www.townsendpress.com

CONTENTS

Reading Selections

TEST BANK   37

Note: There are four mastery tests for each reading skill, supplementing the six mastery tests in the book itself. These tests can be used at a variety of points along the student's path of working through the chapter and the mastery tests in the book.

NOTES FOR INSTRUCTORS

On the first three pages of the Instructor's Editions of *Groundwork for College Reading* and *Groundwork for College Reading with Phonics*, I list some hints for teaching a reading course and for using the book. Here are some additional comments.

Using a Class Contract

In the first class of the semester, I explain to students that I regard the course as a serious, professional relationship between them and me. I say that I want them to sign a professional contract for taking the course. I then pass out a contract for them to read and sign.

In my experience, the contract helps motivate younger students in particular to come to class and to assume responsibility for their own learning. Some of the older students don't need such a contract, but they welcome a clear presentation of basic ground rules regarding attendance and grading in the course.

A copy of the contract appears on pages 6–7; you have permission to modify and use this contract in whatever way you see fit.

Supplements for the Books

There are three supplements for each book:

1 An *Instructor's Edition,* which is identical to the student book except that it provides the answers to all of the practices and tests, as well as explanations of the answers.
2 The combined *Instructor's Manual and Test Bank,* which you are now reading.
3 *Online exercises* consisting of two additional mastery tests for each reading skill plus two combined-skills tests—at least 20 tests in all. These online tests are free for students and instructors using the book and may be accessed at **www.townsendpress.com**.

If you've adopted the book for use in your reading classes, you're entitled to free copies of the two print supplements. Call 1-800-772-6410, send a fax on school letterhead to 1-800-225-8894, or e-mail us at **cs@townsendpress.com** to get them shipped out to you immediately.

A Suggested Syllabus

Weeks 1–10 (Groundwork for College Reading) *or 1–13* (Groundwork . . . with Phonics):

One way to begin using the book is to have students work through the activities in "How to Become a Better Reader and Thinker" on pages 1–6. Then, as the first homework assignment, ask them to read the first twelve pages of "Getting Started" (pages 9–20 in *Groundwork*; pages 143–154 in *Groundwork with Phonics*) and answer the questions. In the next class, finish the chapter and discuss some of the questions students have answered as well as the ones in Review Test 3 on "A Parent Gets a Reading Lesson."

I suggest then teaching one chapter a week, following the order in the book. Generally at the end of a chapter I give two mastery tests: one for practice and one that counts for a grade.

I go over the tests in class right after students take them. (I recommend collecting test papers as students finish and distributing them to students in other parts of the room. Some students resist putting X's on a paper that belongs to the person sitting right next to them.) That way students get immediate feedback on how they have done. Also, after class all I need to do is to check the grades quickly and transfer them to my grade book.

As the semester progresses, I use additional mastery tests, every so often, to review previous skills covered in the class.

Weeks 11–15 (Groundwork for College Reading) or 14–15 (Groundwork . . . with Phonics):

In the remaining weeks, students read two selections a week from Part II, "Ten Reading Selections" (*Groundwork*) or Part III, "Five Reading Selections" (*Groundwork with Phonics*). They also do the remaining mastery tests, including some of the tests in this manual, as well as the combined-skills tests in the book and in this manual.

Having done all of the reading of the materials in the book, as well as all of the thinking required to complete the many activities, students are, in my experience, better readers and thinkers. They are better equipped both to handle a standardized reading test at the semester's end and to go on to content courses in their college curriculum.

Suggested Answers to the Discussion Questions

Pages 23–36 in this manual provide suggested answers to the discussion questions that follow each of the long readings in Parts I and II of *Groundwork* or Parts I, II, and III of *Groundwork with Phonics*. There was simply no room in the Instructor's Edition for this material.

Writing Assignments

Writing and reading are closely related skills: practice at one will make a student better at the other. Also, writing about a selection is an excellent way of thinking about it. For these reasons, two writing assignments are provided (in the Appendixes to the book) for each of the long reading selections.

If you ask students to write about a selection, I suggest you first have them read the "Brief Guide to Effective Writing" that appears on pages 473–474 of *Groundwork* and pages 553–554 of *Groundwork with Phonics*.

Teaching Vocabulary

One basic change that I've made in my teaching of reading is that I now directly teach vocabulary. We all know that students don't know enough words. Because they don't, they have trouble understanding what they read, and they're limited in what they can write. (We have all seen how, in standardized reading tests, students are frustrated because they don't know enough of the words in a passage to understand it and to answer comprehension questions about it. And we all know that because of the vocabulary problem, the standardized tests that are intended to measure reading comprehension are often in fact serving as vocabulary tests.)

I teach vocabulary using a words-in-context approach (it is of no value to ask students to memorize isolated lists of vocabulary words). Specifically, I use a book titled *Groundwork for a Better Vocabulary*, by Beth Johnson, Carole Mohr, and Janet M. Goldstein. There are thirty chapters in this book, with ten words in each chapter. I do the first chapter in class, so that students understand how to use the pronunciation key for the words and see just how the chapter works. I then assign two chapters a week for homework.

In class each week, I walk around and check students' books to make sure that they have worked through the four pages of material for each chapter. (After this quick check, I then return the focus of the class to reading skills.) Every few weeks, I give students one of the several tests that follow each unit of five chapters in the book. My vocabulary syllabus looks like this:

Week 1:   Vocabulary chapter 1 covered in class; chapter 2 assigned for homework
Week 2:   Vocabulary chapters 3–4 for homework
Week 3:   Vocabulary chapters 5–6 for homework plus a test on Unit One in class
Week 4:   Vocabulary chapters 7–8 for homework
Week 5:   Vocabulary chapters 9–10 for homework plus a test on Unit Two in class
Week 6:   Vocabulary chapters 11–12 for homework

Week 7:   Vocabulary chapters 13–14 for homework
Week 8:   Vocabulary chapters 15–16 for homework plus a test on Unit Three in class
Week 9:   Vocabulary chapters 17–18 for homework
Week 10:   Vocabulary chapters 19–20 for homework plus a test on Unit Four in class
Week 11:   Vocabulary chapters 21–22 for homework
Week 12:   Vocabulary chapters 23–24 for homework
Week 13:   Vocabulary chapters 25–26 for homework plus a test on Unit Five in class
Week 14:   Vocabulary chapters 27–28 for homework
Week 15:   Vocabulary chapters 29–30 for homework plus a test on Unit Six in class

The Importance of Continual Reading and Thinking

Continual reading—coupled with thinking about what one has read—is the very heart of a reading class. *Your students will improve their reading and thinking skills only if you guide their reading and thinking.* This statement is emphasized with good reason. If a teacher is not careful, he or she may play too participatory a role in the classroom, getting more reading and thinking practice than the student does. The teacher should serve as a manager, using the materials in the text to give students the skills practice they need. Both *Groundwork for College Reading* and *Groundwork for College Reading with Phonics* help the teacher ensure that students do a great deal of active reading and thinking in the classroom.

The Importance of Constant Feedback

Along with continual reading, writing, and thinking, it is vital that students get frequent feedback. Here are ways they can secure such feedback:

- Small-group interactions
- Class discussions and reviews
- Short one-on-one sessions with the instructor
- Graded quizzes and tests
- The Limited Answer Key in the back of the book
- The online exercises available at **www.townsendpress.com**

In addition, since instructors using *Groundwork for College Reading* or *Groundwork for College Reading with Phonics* as a class text are permitted to reproduce any or all parts of this manual, you can selectively hand out copies of answers included here.

All of the exercises in the books are designed to make it easy to give clear and specific feedback. If students are going to learn to read and think more effectively, then they need clear, logical, specific responses to their efforts. The books and this *Instructor's Manual* enable teachers to provide such feedback.

Outlining and Mapping

To take thoughtful, effective study notes, students need to learn two essential techniques: outlining and mapping. Both techniques often require students to identify the main idea and the major supporting details of a selection. But while educators agree that these techniques are important for students to learn, they are all too seldom taught.

The books give students instruction and practice in both techniques. Passages in the "Supporting Details" and the two "Signal Words" chapters, as well as all of the reading selections in Part II (*Groundwork*) or Part III (*Groundwork with Phonics*), are followed by an outlining or a mapping activity. To complete these activities, students must look closely at the basic organization of the selection. They must think carefully about what they have read by asking two key questions: "What is the point?" and "What is the support for that point?" As students apply the techniques from one selection to the next and get specific feedback on their efforts, they will develop their ability to think in a clear and logical way.

Readability Levels . . . and Their Limitations

Below are the readability grade levels for the text of *Groundwork* itself and the long reading selections. Because the books have been prepared on a computer, and there are now software programs that determine readability, it has been possible to do a complete readability evaluation for each reading, rather than merely sampling excerpts from the materials.

Please remember, however, that there are limits to the reliability and validity of readability scores. For instance, a readability formula cannot account for such significant factors as student interest, prior knowledge of a subject, the number of examples provided to explain concepts, and the overall clarity and logic of the writing. I respect readability levels, but I also take them with a grain of salt, and I have kept other factors in mind while determining the sequence of readings.

Material	Word Count	Reading Level
Text of *Groundwork*		7
*Phonics and Word Parts**		
1 The Struggle Continues	1026	5
2 A Lesson in Love	757	6
3 Friendship and Living Longer	699	6
4 From Horror to Hope	2081	7
Ten Steps to College Reading		
1 A Parent Gets a Reading Lesson	625	5
2 Discovering Words	538	8
3 One Less Sucker Lives	595	6
4 Classroom Notetaking	1232	6
5 Winning the Job Interview Game	966	7
6 Learning Survival Skills	2198	6
7 Migrant Child to College Woman	3710	5
8 Life Over Death	1233	5
9 Dare to Think Big	1038	7
10 Why We Shop	838	6
Reading Selections		
1 Learning to Read: The Marvel Kretzmann Story	2653	6
2 Tickets to Nowhere**	708	6
3 The Fist, the Clay, and the Rock	1014	5
4 A Brother's Lesson **	951	5
5 Joe Davis	2257	5
6 Rosa: A Success Story	1439	6
7 The Lady, or the Tiger?	1089	5
8 Dawn's Story**	4412	7
9 Knowledge Is Power**	2445	8
10 A Love Affair with Books**	1311	8

*This section appears only in *Groundwork for College Reading with Phonics*.

**This selection appears only in *Groundwork for College Reading*.

A Final Note

Writing a book that contains hundreds of explanations and activities is a bit like being in a ball game where one steps up to the plate an almost countless number of times. One tries to get as many hits and extra-base hits as possible: to explain every concept so that students really understand it; to provide readings and practices that both interest students and teach the skills. One tries not to hit any foul balls.

Realistically, though, you might find that despite my best efforts, some items may not work. If they don't, and/or if you or your students are confused or uncertain about certain items, let me know so that I can consider making changes in the next printing or revision of *Groundwork*. Send a note to me at Townsend Press, 439 Kelley Drive, West Berlin, NJ 08091. Alternatively, call Townsend Press at its toll-free number, 1-800-772-6410; send a fax to 1-800-225-8894; or send e-mail to **cs@townsendpress.com**; your comments will be passed on to me. And if you have a question, a Townsend editor will get back to you with an answer very shortly.

My thanks in advance for your help in my effort to keep improving the TP books!

John Langan

A PROFESSIONAL CONTRACT

FOR FIFTEEN WEEKS TOGETHER

between

_____

(Student's name here)

and

_____

(Instructor's name here)

Welcome to *(name of course)* _____. Counting today, we will be spending fifteen weeks together. How successful we are will depend on how well we follow a business contract that I would like you to read and sign, and that I will then sign and return to you. Here are the terms of the contract.

MY ROLE IN THE CONTRACT

My role will be to help you practice and master important reading and writing and thinking and learning skills. I will try to present these communication skills clearly and to give you interesting and worthwhile practice materials. I will conduct this as a skills course—not a lecture course where you could borrow a friend's notes afterward. Typically several skills will be explained briefly in class, and you will then spend most of the class time practicing those skills, making them your own. You will be learning in the best possible way: through doing.

Why learn these skills?

I promise you that the skills will be of real value to you in all the other courses you take in college. They will make you a better reader, writer, thinker, and learner, and they can dramatically increase your chance for success in school.

The skills can be just as valuable for the career work you are likely to do in the future. Consider that America is no longer an industrial society where many people work on farms or in factories. Instead, most jobs now involve providing services or processing information. More than ever, communication skills are the tools of our trade. This course will be concerned directly with helping you learn and strengthen the communication skills that will be vital for job success in the 21st century.

YOUR ROLE IN THE CONTRACT

Experiencing the course

Your role in this contract will be to come to every class and to give your full effort. Much of the value and meaning of this skills course will come from what happens in class, so you must be here on a steady basis. Imagine trying to learn another skill without being present: for example, imagine learning how to drive without the *experience* of actually being in the car and working with the controls and getting feedback from your instructor. How much would you learn about the skill of driving if you relied only on the notes of a classmate? In a similar way, to really learn communication skills, you need direct experience and practice. So if you miss classes, you are, in effect, missing the course.

6

Shaping your attitude

Some people start college with a "high-school mindset." They are passive; they do the minimum they need to get by; their attention is elsewhere; they are like the living dead—and the American high-school system (and watching thousands of hours of television) may be to blame. Gradually these people realize that college is not high school: they don't have to be in college, and they are no longer part of the sad game played out in many high schools, where they receive a free ride and promotion no matter how little they do.

If your attitude about learning has been hurt by what happened in high school, then part of your role is to change your attitude. You can do so, and this contract will help.

Understanding sick days and personal days

You should try not to miss *any* classes. But in the professional environment of this class, like in the work world, everyone is entitled to a set number of sick days as well as "personal days"—unexplained absences. In this course, you will have a total of *(insert number)* _____ such days—which can cover such real-world happenings as sickness, car breakdowns, or even the death of someone you know. If you missed more than this amount of time in a real-world job contract, you would be let go. (Only in some extraordinary situation, such as an extended illness confirmed by a doctor's report, might an exception apply.) The professional terms of the work world will apply here: if you miss more than _____ classes, you cannot pass the course.

YOUR ROLE IF YOU MISS CLASS

If you do miss a class, you are responsible for getting the homework assignment for the following week's class. To do so, call a classmate. Write down the names and phone numbers of two people in the room. (For now, use the people sitting on either side of you; you can always change these names later.)

Classmate # 1: *Name* _____   *Phone* _____

Classmate # 2: *Name* _____   *Phone* _____

Note that you **must** turn in all homework assignments, or you **cannot pass the course**.

If a test or tests are given on a day you miss class, you cannot ordinarily make up these tests. Instead, you will receive a grade of M (Missing) for each missed test. When all your grades are averaged at the end of the semester, three M's will be omitted; the rest will convert to zeros.

YOUR COMMITMENT

I've read this contract, and the terms seem fair to me. (I like the fact that this college class is being treated as a professional situation, and I'm learning the ground rules up front.) I accept the responsibility and the challenge to make this course worth my time and money.

_____   _____

Signed by (your name here)   *Date*

_____

Witnessed by the instructor

OR: If you don't want to sign this, please meet with me after this class to talk about why.

ANSWERS TO THE TESTS IN THE BOOK

Answers to the Review and Mastery Tests in "Phonics and Word Parts"

CONSONANTS:
Review Test 1
1. B
2. A
3. B
4. B

CONSONANTS:
Review Test 2

A.
1. come
2. curse
3. cut
4. gun
5. hug

B.
6. bribe
7. found
8. smile
9. stain
10. unplug

C.
11. Ketchup
12. Elephants
13. flashing
14. cough
15. truth

D.
16. bitten
17. reign
18. truck
19. whole
20. wrong

CONSONANTS:
Review Test 3
1. A
2. C
3. B
4. A
5. A
6. C
7. B
8. B
9. C
10. A

CONSONANTS:
Mastery Test 1

A.
1. hard **c**
2. soft **c**
3. hard **g**
4. soft **g**
5. hard **g**

B.
6. strange
7. found
8. professor
9. grave
10. brief

C.
11. enough
12. Joseph
13. pamphlet
14. she
15. think

D.
16. Knitting
17. dumb
18. wristband
19. stuck
20. sitting

CONSONANTS:
Mastery Test 2

A.
1. cabbage
2. gold
3. castles
4. North Carolina
5. great people

B.
6. glad
7. grin
8. prank
9. skill
10. slim

C.
11. Phil
12. this
13. enough
14. showroom
15. check

D. (16–25.)

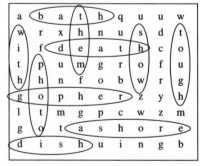

CONSONANTS:
Mastery Test 3

A.
1. hard **g**
2. soft **c**
3. soft **g**
4. soft **c**
5. hard **c**

B.
6. surprise
7. created
8. small
9. breed
10. lands

C.
11. knob
12. limb
13. pudding
14. sack
15. wrist

D. (16–25.)

CONSONANTS:
Mastery Test 4

A. 1. recent   4. ages
2. concert   5. stage
3. price

B. (6–15.)

```
h o h o s t a m p
u f t x n w h y s
n b r i e f n k f
t h i s e v n t a
i o p b z x s l i
s k a t e f r q n
k a t r o u n d t
b l u s h i h e r
r u s p e c i a l
```

C. 16. cheap   **D.** 21. write
17. flush   22. well-known
18. phase   23. wholly
19. rough   24. wrong
20. thousand   25. with luck

CONSONANTS:
Mastery Test 5

A. 1. ace   **C.** 11. fish
2. civil   12. graph
3. procedures   13. chef
4. vegetation   14. laugh
5. principal   15. thought

B. 6. softly   **D.** 16. fall
7. respected   17. dumb
8. spanked   18. knocking
9. strong   19. running a
10. bump   fever
                 20. thumb

CONSONANTS:
Mastery Test 6

A. 1. public   **C.** 11. accomplish
2. countless   12. chance
3. Canada   13. enough
4. gained   14. philosophy
5. soccer   15. rich

B. 6. Fred   **D.** 16. known
7. bank   17. horrible
8. start   18. shopping
9. sandwich   19. shocking
10. one hundred   20. whole lot

VOWELS:
Review Test 1

1. B
2. T
3. C
4. B

VOWELS:
Review Test 2

A. 1. cram   6. file
2. place   7. nod
3. dress   8. home
4. green   9. dust
5. mix   10. used

B. 11. Silent **e**; the **a** is long and the **e** is silent
12. Final Single Vowel; the single **o** at the end is long
13. Two Vowels Together; the **o** is long, and the **a** is silent
14. Two Vowels Together; the **e** is long, and the **a** is silent
15. Silent **e**; the **a** is long, and the **e** is silent

C. 16. ī; at end of one-syllable word
17. ē; at end of word with more than one syllable
18. ĭ; in middle of first syllable
19. ē; at end of word with more than one syllable
20. ī; at end of one-syllable word

VOWELS:
Review Test 3

1. A   6. C
2. A   7. C
3. A   8. B
4. C   9. B
5. C   10. C

VOWELS:
Mastery Test 1

A.
1. grant
2. stage
3. tent
4. three
5. skip
6. slide
7. not
8. rope
9. stun
10. cute

B.
11. Silent **e**; the **o** is long and the **e** is silent
12. Final Single Vowel; the **e** is long
13. Two Vowels Together; the **e** is long, and the **a** is silent
14. Silent **e**; the **a** is long, and the **e** is silent
15. Two Vowels Together; the **o** is long, and the **a** is silent

C.
16. ī; at end of one-syllable word
17. ē; at end of word with more than one syllable
18. ĭ; in middle of first syllable
19. ī; at end of one-syllable word
20. ē; at end of word with more than one syllable

VOWELS:
Mastery Test 2

A.
1. ē
2. ĭ
3. r
4. ĕ
5. ŭ
6. ŏ
7. ā
8. ī
9. ū
10. r

B.
11. drop
12. ten
13. sap
14. run
15. brick

C.
16. snake
17. wrote
18. soap
19. treat
20. hi

D.
21. long **oo**
22. short **oo**
23. long **oo**
24. short **oo**
25. long **oo**

VOWELS:
Mastery Test 3

A.

1. add
2. flat
3. bench
4. smell
5. chin
6. quilt
7. plod
8. clock
9. nun
10. stuff

B.
11. speedy
12. Jake
13. float
14. easy
15. place

C.
16. long **e**
17. long **i**
18. short **i**
19. long **e**
20. long **i**

D.
21. looking; short **oo**
22. bedroom; long **oo**
23. toothpaste; long **oo**
24. shampoo; long **oo**
25. tools; long **oo**

VOWELS:
Mastery Test 4

A.

1. claim
2. stain
3. cheese
4. sweet
5. glide
6. wise
7. boat
8. toast
9. cute
10. use

B.
11. wilt
12. Montana
13. half
14. sister
15. west

C.
16. Two Vowels Together
17. Silent **e**
18. Final Single Vowel
19. Two Vowels Together
20. Two Vowels Together
21. Silent **e**
22. Final Single Vowel
23. Silent **e**
24. Two Vowels Together
25. Two Vowels Together

VOWELS:
Mastery Test 5

A.
1. apple
2. swims
3. under
4. events
5. expand
11. A
12. goad
13. B
14. yo-yo
15. C

B.
6. peaceful
7. B
8. nine
9. A
10. race

C.
16. myths

D.
17. sly
18. dry

E.
19. Surely
20. carry

VOWELS:
Mastery Test 6

A.
1. hunt
2. little
3. six
4. nest
5. vast

B.
6. five
7. these
8. main
9. coast
10. east
11. we
12. fish
13. Yet
14. west
15. world

C.
16. too; long **oo**
17. food; long **oo**
18. cook; short **oo**
19. football; short **oo**
20. hook; short **oo**

SYLLABLES:
Review Test 1
1. T
2. B
3. A
4. T

SYLLABLES:
Review Test 2
A.
2. sys-tem, 1
3. fo-cus, 2
4. com-ment, 1
5. mu-sic, 2
6. si-lent, 2
7. lec-ture, 1
8. im-por-tant, 1, 1
9. pri-va-cy, 2, 2
10. at-tor-ney, 1, 1

B.
12. pay-ment, 4
13. sam-ple, 3
14. sail-boat, 5
15. trou-ble, 3
16. joy-ful, 4
17. bot-tle, 3
18. re-place-ment, 4, 4
19. non-smok-er, 4, 4
20. dis-a-ble, 4, 3

SYLLABLES:
Review Test 3
1. C
2. A
3. B
4. B
5. B
6. C
7. B
8. A
9. C
10. B

SYLLABLES:
Mastery Test 1
A.
1. for-ward, 1
2. oc-cur, 1
3. mo-tive, 2
4. wel-come, 1
5. u-nite, 2
6. so-da, 2

B.
7. crip-ple, 3
8. glad-ly, 4
9. hall-way, 5
10. dis-trust, 4
11. puz-zle, 3
12. cloud-burst, 5
13. good-ness, 4

C.
14. field-house
15. break-down
16. side-walk
17. land-slide

D.
18. bad-ly
19. de-layed
20. move-ment

SYLLABLES:
Mastery Test 2
A.
1. en-ter-tain   1, 1
2. dip-lo-mat   1, 2
3. ab-so-lute   1, 2
4. hi-ber-nate   2, 1
5. al-co-hol   1, 2
6. ter-mi-nal   1, 2

B.
7. un-friend-ly   4, 4
8. out-field-er   5, 4
9. pre-view-ing   4, 4
10. rat-tle-snake   3, 5
11. new-ly-wed   4, 5
12. grand-moth-er   5, 4
13. puz-zle-ment   3, 4

C.
14. pre-view
15. re-fold-ed
16. skill-ful
17. in-struc-tion
18. day-break
19. path-way
20. school-room

SYLLABLES:
Mastery Test 3
A.
1. to-ma-to   2, 2
2. in-cu-bate   4, 2
3. dis-con-nect   4, 1
4. sin-cere-ly   1, 4
5. re-search-er   4, 4
6. an-kle-bone   3, 5
7. so-lu-tion   2, 4
8. be-long-ing   2, 4
9. house-keep-ing   5, 4
10. pho-to-graph   2, 5

B.
11. cup-board
12. nee-dle-point
13. earth-quakes
14. com-mon-place
15. fire-fight-er

C.
16. A
17. C
18. A
19. B
20. B

SYLLABLES:
Mastery Test 4
A.
1. out-stand-ing   5, 4
2. re-ar-range   4, 1
3. set-tle-ment   3, 4
4. in-cor-rect   4, 1
5. fol-low-ing   1, 4
6. glass-mak-er   5, 4
7. e-lec-tron   2, 1
8. ex-pen-sive   4, 1
9. han-dle-bar   3, 5
10. pil-low-case   1, 5

B.
11. rid-dle
12. ter-ri-ble
13. hor-ri-ble
14. un-a-ble
15. pos-si-ble

C.
16. ad-just-ing
17. dis-be-liev-ing
18. de-sign-er
19. de-vo-tion
20. pre-vent-a-ble

D.
21. B
22. C
23. C
24. A
25. B

SYLLABLES:
Mastery Test 5
A.
1. non-ru-ral   4, 2
2. cheese-burg-er   5, 4
3. un-law-ful   4, 4
4. sun-bon-net   5, 1
5. moun-tain-top   1, 5
6. flame-throw-er   5, 4
7. mo-tor-bike   2, 5
8. be-lit-tle   2, 3
9. o-pen-ing   2, 4
10. chair-per-son   5, 1

B.
11. un-ex-pect-ed-ly
12. dis-cov-ered
13. un-pro-mis-ing
14. un-be-liev-a-ble
15. ex-haust-ing

C.
16. com-put-er
17. ex-er-cise
18. fol-low-ing
19. Fi-nal-ly
20. im-prove-ment

SYLLABLES:
Mastery Test 6
A.
1. prin-ci-pal   1, 2
2. ex-ter-nal   4, 1
3. Es-ki-mo   1, 2
4. re-volv-er   4, 4
5. can-ni-bal   1, 2
6. mar-ket-place   1, 5
7. con-vic-tion   4, 4
8. rep-ri-mand   1, 2
9. va-can-cy   2, 1
10. card-hold-er   5, 4

B.
11. pre-scrip-tion
12. re-lax-ing
13. un-like-ly
14. com-plete-ly

C.
16. re-veal-ing
17. re-cent-ly
18. sur-pris-ing
19. ex-plain-ing
20. con-fi-dence
18. phy-si-cians

WORD PARTS:
Review Test 1
1. B
2. B
3. C
4. C

WORD PARTS:
Review Test 2
1. predicted
2. including
3. refinement
4. submerge
5. visible
6. expelled
7. telephoto
8. biology
9. Hinduism
10. spectacles

WORD PARTS:
Review Test 3
1. C
2. C
3. B
4. C
5. A
6. A
7. B
8. B
9. A
10. C

WORD PARTS:
Mastery Test 1
1. researcher
2. unclean
3. autobiography
4. expand
5. pedal
6. monologue
7. benefits
8. registration
9. refresh
10. convention

WORD PARTS:
Mastery Test 2
1. inspect
2. telephone
3. include
4. useful
5. Similarly
6. specialists
7. extracted
8. killers
9. identification
10. reconsider

WORD PARTS:
Mastery Test 3
1. audience
2. seriously
3. telescope
4. misplaced
5. preoccupied
6. portable
7. monotone
8. superior
9. substandard
10. devilish

WORD PARTS:
Mastery Test 4
1. preparing
2. spectacle
3. inside
4. beautiful
5. manage
6. audible
7. eagerly
8. amazement
9. extremely
10. replied

WORD PARTS:
Mastery Test 5
A.
1. penniless
2. humorists
3. vegetarianism
4. biochemistry
5. porter

B.
6. careful
7. Unfortunately
8. breeder
9. substandard
10. inspect

WORD PARTS:
Mastery Test 6
A.
1. unloved
2. podiatrist
3. prejudge
4. flexible
5. teleconference

B.
6. reacquaint
7. successful
8. strapless
9. confidently
10. post-high-school

Answers to the Review and Mastery Tests in "Ten Steps to College Reading"

GETTING STARTED:
Review Test 1
1. B
2. A
3. D
4. C

GETTING STARTED:
Review Test 2

Answers will vary.

GETTING STARTED:
Review Test 3
1. A   6. D
2. D   7. A
3. B   8. B
4. D   9. D
5. C   10. A

GETTING STARTED:
Mastery Test 1

Answers will vary.

GETTING STARTED:
Mastery Test 2

Answers will vary.

GETTING STARTED:
Mastery Test 3

Answers will vary.

Note: As opposed to those in later chapters, the six mastery tests in this chapter are ungraded. The object is not to test information or skills, but to reinforce the importance of the student's attitude, basic study skills, and reading.

GETTING STARTED:
Mastery Test 4

Answers will vary.

GETTING STARTED:
Mastery Test 5

Answers will vary.

GETTING STARTED:
Mastery Test 6

Answers will vary.

DICTIONARY USE:
Review Test 1
1. B
2. A
3. T
4. D

DICTIONARY USE:
Review Test 2
A. 1. C
    2. C
B. 3. business
    4. visitor
    5. surprise
    6. really
C. 7. mi•cro•scope / mī′krə-skōp′
    8. pro•nun•ci•a•tion /
       prə′nŭn-sē-ā′shən
D. 9. B
   10. A

DICTIONARY USE:
Review Test 3
Dictionary Questions
1. C   6. five; second
2. C   7. adjective
3. B   8. *Answers to*
4. B   9. *items 8–10*
5. unavoidable   10. *will vary.*

Questions about the Reading
1. A   6. A
2. C   7. D
3. A   8. B
4. D   9. A
5. D   10. A

DICTIONARY USE:
Mastery Test 1
A. 1. B
    2. C
B. 3. bicycle
    4. taking
    5. hurry
    6. believe
C. 7. cir•cum•stance / sûr′kəm-stăns′
    8. in•sig•nif•i•cant /
       ĭn′sĭg-nĭf′ĭ-kənt
D. 9. she
   10. sit

DICTIONARY USE:
Mastery Test 2
A. 1. B
    2. A
B. 3. label
    4. frown
    5. action
    6. orderly
C. 7. en•er•get•ic / ĕn′ər-jĕt′ĭk
    8. dem•on•stra•tion /
       dĕm′ən-strā′shən
D. 9. hi
   10. hat

DICTIONARY USE:
Mastery Test 3
A. 1. A
    2. A
B. 3. decide
    4. complete
C. 5. fun•da•men•tal / fŭn′də-mĕn′tl
    6. ap•prox•i•mate /
       ə-prŏk′sə-mĭt (**or** ə-prŏk′sə-māt′)
D. 7. hat
    8. go
    9. sit
   10. hi

DICTIONARY USE:
Mastery Test 4

1. A	6. B
2. B	7. 4
3. A	8. A
4. 2	9. 2
5. 1	10. 5

DICTIONARY USE:
Mastery Test 5

1. A	6. B
2. B	7. 4
3. A	8. A
4. 1	9. 3
5. 2	10. 1

DICTIONARY USE:
Mastery Test 6

A.
1. B	6. B
2. B	7. 3
3. C	8. A
4. 3	9. 2
5. 1	10. 1

B. 11. instructor
12. practice
13. receive
14. impression
15. easy

C. 16. ab•rupt / ə-brŭpt′
17. fa•tigue / fə-tēg′
18. ex•trav•a•gant / ĭk-străv′ə-gənt
19. es•sen•tial / ĭ-sĕn′shəl
20. mis•in•ter•pret / mĭs′ĭn-tûr′prĭt

VOCABULARY IN CONTEXT:
Review Test 1

1. C
2. A
3. C
4. A

VOCABULARY IN CONTEXT:
Review Test 2

A.
1. A	6. B

B.
2. C	7. A
3. B	8. C
4. A	9. B
5. B	10. B

VOCABULARY IN CONTEXT:
Review Test 3

Vocabulary in Context Questions

1. B	6. C
2. B	7. A
3. C	8. D
4. A	9. C
5. D	10. D

Questions about the Reading

1. D	6. D
2. C	7. A
3. C	8. A
4. B	9. B
5. C	10. C

VOCABULARY IN CONTEXT:
Mastery Test 1

A. 1. *Examples:* scribbling instead of taking notes, constantly looking at the clock, writing messages to one another; A
2. *Examples:* swimming, jogging, biking; C
3. *Examples:* nodding, shaking their heads; C

B. 4. suitable
5. honest
6. greatest

C. 7. *Antonym:* simple; C
8. *Antonym:* dishonest; D

D. 9. B
10. B

VOCABULARY IN CONTEXT:
Mastery Test 2

A. 1. *Examples:* the deserts of Arizona, the wilderness of Alaska; D
2. *Examples:* height, eye color, hair color; A
3. *Examples:* fall backwards, move sideways; B

B. 4. understand
5. makes them better people
6. changed

C. 7. *Antonym:* truth; B
8. *Antonym:* sleepy; D

D. 9. A
10. A

VOCABULARY IN CONTEXT:
Mastery Test 3

1. B	6. B
2. A	7. B
3. C	8. C
4. B	9. A
5. C	10. C

VOCABULARY IN CONTEXT:
Mastery Test 4

1.	D	6.	B
2.	B	7.	C
3.	A	8.	A
4.	C	9.	C
5.	A	10.	A

VOCABULARY IN CONTEXT:
Mastery Test 5

A. 1. C   **B.** 6. A
     2. C   7. D
     3. B   8. C
     4. A   9. B
     5. B   10. A

VOCABULARY IN CONTEXT:
Mastery Test 6

A. 1. C   **B.** 6. B
     2. A   7. B
     3. C   8. C
     4. B   9. B
     5. A   10. B

MAIN IDEAS:
Review Test 1

1. specific
2. main idea
3. topic
4. T

MAIN IDEAS:
Review Test 2

A. 1. relative
     2. flavor
     3. game
     4. footwear

B. *(Answers will vary. Below are samples.)*
   5–6. boat, plane
   7–8. drum, piano

C. *Group 1*   *Group 2*
     A. MI   A. SD
     B. SD   B. SD
     C. T   C. MI
     D. SD   D. T

D. *Paragraph 1*   *Paragraph 2*
   17. B   19. B
   18. 1   20. 2

MAIN IDEAS:
Review Test 3

1.	A	6.	A
2.	D	7.	D
3.	B	8.	C
4.	A	9.	B
5.	C	10.	A

MAIN IDEAS:
Mastery Test 1

A. 1. music
     2. household appliance
     3. cook
     4. protection
     5. city
     6. crime
     7. metal
     8. newspaper

B. *(Answers will vary. Below are samples.)*
   9–10. ham and cheese, tuna salad
  11–12. Smokey Robinson,
         Carrie Underwood
  13–14. rose, carnation
  15–16. hammer, saw
  17–18. rugs, tile
  19–20. Oprah, Howard Stern

MAIN IDEAS:
Mastery Test 2

A. 1. hat
     2. cereal
     3. debt
     4. minor problems
     5. card game
     6. monster
     7. fabric
     8. time savers

B. *(Answers will vary. Below are samples.)*
   9–10. pear, orange
  11–12. hockey, soccer
  13–14. taking a walk, sunbathing
  15–16. aspirin, Tylenol
  17–18. cash, debit card
  19–20. loud noises, overwork

MAIN IDEAS:
Mastery Test 3

Group 1   *Group 4*
A. MI   A. MI
B. T   B. SD
C. SD   C. T
D. SD   D. SD

Group 2   *Group 5*
A. SD   A. SD
B. MI   B. MI
C. SD   C. SD
D. T   D. T

Group 3
A. SD
B. T
C. SD
D. MI

MAIN IDEAS:
Mastery Test 4

A. 1. C   **D.** 7. B
     2. 1   8. 1
B. 3. B   **E.** 9. C
     4. 1   10. 2
C. 5. A
     6. 2

MAIN IDEAS:
Mastery Test 5

A. 1. B   **D.** 7. B
     2. 1   8. 1
B. 3. A   **E.** 9. C
     4. 1   10. 6
C. 5. C
     6. 2

MAIN IDEAS:
Mastery Test 6

A. 1. B   **D.** 7. B
     2. 2   8. 2
B. 3. A   **E.** 9. B
     4. 6   10. 1
C. 5. A
     6. 1

SUPPORTING DETAILS:
Review Test 1
1. main idea (**or** main point)
2. map
3. B
4. A

(*Note: Wording of answers to the outline and map questions in these tests may vary.*)

SUPPORTING DETAILS:
Mastery Test 1
A. *Group 1*   *Group 2*
1. SD   1. MI
2. MI   2. SD
3. SD   3. SD

B. 7. 1. They need the money.
8. 2. They like working.
9. first
10. other

SUPPORTING DETAILS:
Mastery Test 4
A. (1–4.)
Main idea: . . . the major causes of heart disease.
• High cholesterol
• High blood pressure
• Inactivity

5. major causes (of heart disease)

B. (6–10.)
1a. If the story is imaginary, start with "Once upon a time . . ."
2. Have a setting for your story.
2b. For a nonfiction story, say something like "outside of town."
3. Appeal to the senses.
3a. Describe how things look.

SUPPORTING DETAILS:
Review Test 2
A. 1. They use eye contact.
2. They use head and face motions.
 b. Smiling or nodding can show acceptance.
3. They use hand movements.
 a. Upraised hands can show positive emphasis.
 b. A clenched fist can show anger.

B. 7. several ways
8. For one thing
9. another
10. Finally

SUPPORTING DETAILS:
Mastery Test 2
A. *Group 1*   *Group 2*
1. SD   1. SD
2. SD   2. MI
3. MI   3. SD

B. 7. 1. Cremation
8. 2. Natural burial
9. 3. Donating your body to science
10. Another

SUPPORTING DETAILS:
Mastery Test 5
A. (1–4.)
• Don't yell a lot at children.
• Don't make too many rules.
• Don't show a child disrespect.
• Don't neglect to acknowledge good behavior.

B. (5–10.)
1. Dishonesty
1b. Stealing
2. Irresponsibility
2a. Taking too many breaks
3a. Frequent absences
3b. Lateness

SUPPORTING DETAILS:
Review Test 3
1. C
2. C
3. B
4. C
5. A
6. A
7–10. *Main idea:* There are ways to do well at job interviews.
2. Plan to arrive at the interview a few minutes early.
4a. Tell me about yourself.
4g. What are your greatest strengths?

SUPPORTING DETAILS:
Mastery Test 3
A. 1. C   **B.** 6. A
2. C   7. third
3. A   8. B
4. B   9. C
5. B   10. B

SUPPORTING DETAILS:
Mastery Test 6
A. 1. B
2. C
3. B
4. B
5. B

B. (6–10.)
• The brain is firm and grey.
• New brain cells can't be created once cells have been damaged or lost.
• Humans use only 10 percent of their brains.
• There are "left brain" and "right brain" abilities.

10. several incorrect ideas

FINDING MAIN IDEAS:
Review Test 1
1. first
2. main idea
3. *but*
4. end

FINDING MAIN IDEAS:
Review Test 2
1. 2
2. 1
3. 3
4. 1

FINDING MAIN IDEAS:
Review Test 3
1. B   6. D
2. C   7. B
3. B   8. D
4. A   9. A
5. A   10. D

FINDING MAIN IDEAS:
Mastery Test 1
1. 1   4. 3
2. 6   5. 2
3. 2

FINDING MAIN IDEAS:
Mastery Test 2
1. 2   4. 7
2. 1   5. 1
3. 2

FINDING MAIN IDEAS:
Mastery Test 3
1. 2   4. 2
2. 1   5. 1
3. 5

FINDING MAIN IDEAS:
Mastery Test 4
1. 1   4. 2
2. 1   5. 2
3. 6

FINDING MAIN IDEAS:
Mastery Test 5
1. 1   4. 2
2. 7   5. 5
3. 1

FINDING MAIN IDEAS:
Mastery Test 6
1. 1   4. 8
2. 3   5. 4
3. 1

SIGNAL WORDS I:
Review Test 1
1. transitions
2. T
3. addition
4. time

SIGNAL WORDS I:
Review Test 2
A.
1. B; also
2. C; finally
3. D; In addition
4. A; After

B.
5. When
6. soon
7. then

C.
8. One
9. Another
10. third

SIGNAL WORDS I:
Review Test 3
1. D   6. B
2. A   7. D
3. C   8. C
4. B   9. B
5. A   10. A

SIGNAL WORDS I:
Mastery Test 1
A.
1. A; also
2. D; until
3. E; While
4. C; In addition
5. B; First of all

B.
6. when
7. then
8. before
9. finally
10. B

SIGNAL WORDS I:
Mastery Test 2
A.
1. A; After
2. B; also
3. E; Second
4. C; During
5. D; Moreover

B.
6. To begin with
7. Next (**or** Then)
8. During
9. Then (**or** Next)
10. Last

SIGNAL WORDS I:
Mastery Test 3
A.
1. One
2. Another

B.
3. first
4. second
5. then
6. Finally

C.
7. For one thing
8. also
9. Furthermore
10. A

SIGNAL WORDS I:
Mastery Test 4
A.
1. during
2. After
3. B

B.
4. One
5. Another
6. A

C.
7. During
8. Then
9. Finally
10. B

SIGNAL WORDS I:
Mastery Test 5
A. 1. A
2–3. *Any two of the following:* First, second, Third, Finally
4–6. *(Wording of answers may vary.)*
1. Be well informed about the work.
2. Work harder than anyone else in the group.
3. Be open to an exchange of ideas with others in the group.

B. 7. A
8–10. *(Wording of answers may vary.)*
• Genes
• Environment
• Too much television

SIGNAL WORDS I:
Mastery Test 6
A. 1. A
2–3. *Any two of the following:* For one thing, secondly, Finally
4–5. *(Wording of answers may vary.)*
1. Attractiveness can change with age.
3. Love sees loveliness.

B. 6. A
7–8. *Any two of the following:* One, Another, third
9–10. *(Wording of answers may vary.)*
• Meet needs
• Exchange information

SIGNAL WORDS II:
Review Test 1
1. idea
2. example
3. contrast
4. cause and effect

SIGNAL WORDS II:
Review Test 2
A. 1. for instance
   2. Therefore
   3. However

B. 4. different
   5. however
   6. For instance
   7. example
   8. such as

C. 9. reason
   10. As a result

SIGNAL WORDS II:
Review Test 3
1. C   6. A
2. B   7. D
3. C   8. C
4. B   9. B
5. C   10. C

SIGNAL WORDS II:
Mastery Test 1
A. 1. B; but
   2. E; so that
   3. C; For instance
   4. D; However
   5. A; As a result

B. 6. lead to
   7. caused
   8. result
   9. due to
   10. C

SIGNAL WORDS II:
Mastery Test 2
A. 1. A; Although
   2. B; Because
   3. C; example
   4. E; Instead
   5. F; reason
   6. D; For instance

B. 7. due to
   8. Conse-
      quently
   9. result
   10. C

SIGNAL WORDS II:
Mastery Test 3
A. 1. however
   2. different
   3. B

B. 4. resulted
   5. Because of
   6. therefore
   7. C

C. 8. For instance
   9. example
   10. A

SIGNAL WORDS II:
Mastery Test 4
A. 1. result in
   2. consequence
   3. Therefore
   4. C

B. 5. on the other hand
   6. while
   7. B

C. 8. For instance
   9. example
   10. A

SIGNAL WORDS II:
Mastery Test 5
A. 1. reason
   2. Because of
   3. lead to
   4. result
   5. so
   6. C

7–9. (*Wording of answers may vary.*)
   1. Poor people live in old, badly maintained buildings with faulty wiring.
   2. The poor rely on open flames for light and heat.
   3. Poor people cannot afford smoke detectors.

B. 10. B

SIGNAL WORDS II:
Mastery Test 6
A. 1. C
2–5. (*Wording of answers may vary.*)
   Main idea: Stress can lead to extreme behaviors.
   1. Drug abuse
   2. Aggression
   3. Depression and suicide attempts

B. 6. A
7–10. (*Wording of answers may vary.*)
   • Extreme fear of germs
     • opening a book or eating a sandwich
   • Constant focus on money
     • where he tried to remove his gold fillings and sell them

INFERENCES:
Review Test 1
1. inferences
2. stated
3. useful
4. main idea

INFERENCES:
Review Test 2
A. (1–2.) 3, 4

B. (3–4.) 1, 4

C. 5. C

INFERENCES:
Review Test 3
1.	B	6.	D
2.	A	7.	A
3.	C	8.	C
4.	B	9.	B
5.	A	10.	B

INFERENCES:
Mastery Test 1
A. (1–3.) A, D, E

B. (4–7.) A, D; F, H

C. (8–10.) B, D, E

INFERENCES:
Mastery Test 2
A. (1–3.) A, C, E

B. (4–7.) A, C; F, H

C. (8–10.) A, D, E

INFERENCES:
Mastery Test 3
A. (1–3.) A, B, E

B. (4–7.) B, C; E, F

C. (8–10.) A, D, E

INFERENCES:
Mastery Test 4
A. (1–2.) A, D

B. (3–4.) A, C

C. 5. B

INFERENCES:
Mastery Test 5
A. (1–2.) A, D
(3–4.) E, G

B. 5. D

INFERENCES:
Mastery Test 6
A. (1–2.) B, D
(3–4.) F, H

B. 5. C

THE BASICS OF ARGUMENT:
Review Test 1
1. main idea
2. support
3. support
4. point

THE BASICS OF ARGUMENT:
Review Test 2
A. (1–4.)
1. A: S
2. B: P
3. C: S
4. D: S

B. 5. B
C. (6–8.) A, B, C
D. (9–10.)
Group 1: B
Group 2: B

THE BASICS OF ARGUMENT:
Review Test 3
1.	B	6.	D
2.	C	7.	B
3.	B	8.	A
4.	A	9.	A
5.	B	10.	B

THE BASICS OF ARGUMENT:
Mastery Test 1

Group 1	Group 3	Group 5
A. P	A. S	A. P
B. S	B. S	B. S
C. S	C. S	C. S
D. S	D. P	D. S

Group 2	Group 4
A. P	A. S
B. S	B. S
C. S	C. P
D. S	D. S

THE BASICS OF ARGUMENT:
Mastery Test 2
A. (1–8.)

Group 1	Group 2
A. S	A. S
B. P	B. S
C. S	C. P
D. S	D. S

B. 9. A

C. 10. D

THE BASICS OF ARGUMENT:
Mastery Test 3
A. 1–3. A, D, E
4–6. B, D, E
7–9. C, D, E

B. 10. B

THE BASICS OF ARGUMENT:
Mastery Test 4
A. (1–8.)

Group 1	Group 2
A. S	A. S
B. S	B. S
C. S	C. S
D. P	D. P

B. 9. B

C. 10. C

THE BASICS OF ARGUMENT:
Mastery Test 5
A. 1–3. A, B, E
4–6. B, C, D
7–9. B, C, E

B. 10. C

THE BASICS OF ARGUMENT:
Mastery Test 6
A. (1–4.)
A. S
B. S
C. P
D. S

B. 5–7. A, C, E

C. 8–10.
Group 1: D
Group 2: D
Group 3: D

Answers to the Reading Selections

1 LEARNING TO READ

Vocabulary Questions

1. B	6. D
2. C	7. A
3. C	8. C
4. A	9. E
5. B	10. B

Comprehension Questions

1. C	6. D
2. A	7. C
3. D	8. A
4. C	9. B
5. A	10. C

Mapping

C, *G*, E, D, B, *A*, F

2 TICKETS TO NOWHERE

Vocabulary Questions

1. B	6. A
2. C	7. C
3. B	8. D
4. B	9. E
5. D	10. B

Comprehension Questions

1. C	6. D
2. A	7. C
3. C	8. C
4. C	9. D
5. C	10. B

Mapping

- Jim quits high school.
- *Jim moves to Florida and takes a job, hoping he'll get lucky there and win the lottery.*
- The Florida lottery jackpot becomes $54 million.
- Jim gets into an automobile accident that costs him much of his weekly salary.
- *Jim doubles the amount of his normal investment in the lottery.*
- The winning lottery number is announced; Jim doesn't win.

3 THE FIST, THE CLAY, AND THE ROCK

Vocabulary Questions

1. A	6. B
2. C	7. C
3. D	8. D
4. B	9. E
5. B	10. A

Comprehension Questions

1. D	6. D
2. B	7. A
3. D	8. A
4. B	9. D
5. A	10. B

Outlining

2. Mr. Gery holds up his fist and asks his class to imagine that it is the real world.
4. Mr. Gery smashes his fist into the lump of clay.
7. Mr. Gery calls students who don't do their work "Mr. Clay" or "Ms. Clay."
8. By the end of the semester, Mr. Gery has to call very few of his students "Mr. or Ms. Clay."

4 A BROTHER'S LESSON

Vocabulary Questions

1. B	6. B
2. D	7. C
3. D	8. E
4. A	9. D
5. B	10. A

Comprehension Questions

1. D	6. C
2. C	7. A
3. C	8. B
4. C	9. D
5. D	10. C

Mapping

- The author's mother is overcome by fumes.
- Oliver is born.
- Oliver's mother finds out that Oliver is blind.
- We learn that Oliver dies.
- Roe feeds Oliver, and de Vinck eventually marries her.

5 JOE DAVIS

Vocabulary Questions

1. C	6. A
2. A	7. B
3. B	8. C
4. A	9. E
5. C	10. D

Comprehension Questions

1. B	6. B
2. A	7. C
3. C	8. D
4. C	9. D
5. A	10. A

Outlining

2. Joe gets shot, which paralyzes him from the chest down.
3. Joe starts selling drugs.
6. Joe takes a job as a receptionist.
8. Joe earns two college degrees.

6 ROSA: A SUCCESS STORY

Vocabulary Questions

1. C	6. B
2. A	7. A
3. A	8. D
4. B	9. E
5. C	10. C

Comprehension Questions

1. B	6. B
2. C	7. C
3. D	8. D
4. C	9. B
5. B	10. A

Mapping

- Rosa's escape to the United States
- Rosa's education toward an associate's degree
- Rosa's graduation and party
- Rosa's education toward a bachelor's degree
- Rosa's visit with the twins

7 THE LADY, OR THE TIGER?

Vocabulary Questions

1. D	6. E
2. B	7. B
3. C	8. A
4. C	9. D
5. D	10. C

Comprehension Questions

1. D	6. D
2. A	7. B
3. B	8. B
4. B	9. A
5. C	10. C

Summarizing

- *Behind one door was a beautiful lady,* whom the accused would marry immediately. It did not matter if he was already married or loved someone else.
- *When the kind found out that the two were seeing each other, he* had the young man arrested and thrown into prison.
- *While this was happening, the princess* learned the secret of the two doors.
- *She had once imagined that* she had seen the girl and her lover look admiringly at each other.
- *He knew* that the princess knew which door hid the lady, and which door hid the tiger.

8 DAWN'S STORY

Vocabulary Questions

1. C	6. B
2. C	7. A
3. C	8. C
4. D	9. D
5. C	10. E

Comprehension Questions

1. B	6. A
2. A	7. A
3. D	8. C
4. C	9. C
5. D	10. B

Outlining

3. Dawn's stepfather Larry beats and rapes her.
6. Dawn meets and marries Den, a factory worker.
9. Den continues to threaten Dawn, so Dawn lets him have the house and moves out.
12. With the help of counseling and Alcoholics Anonymous, Dawn stops drinking.

9 KNOWLEDGE IS POWER

Vocabulary Questions

1. C	6. B
2. B	7. D
3. D	8. E
4. D	9. C
5. C	10. A

Comprehension Questions

1. C	6. A
2. B	7. A
3. B	8. D
4. D	9. C
5. B	10. C

Mapping

- As a high-school student, Anna-Maria is inspired by the words "Knowledge is real power."
- Anna-Maria decides to go to college.
- She decides that going to a special college in the United States would be better than attending the University of Zagreb.
- After much struggle, Anna-Maria and her family find the money needed to get her to the United States.
- Finally in the United States, Anna-Maria has found her new life to be all that she had hoped for.

10 A LOVE AFFAIR WITH BOOKS

Vocabulary Questions

1. D	6. B
2. A	7. C
3. D	8. D
4. A	9. E
5. C	10. A

Comprehension Questions

1. B	6. C
2. B	7. C, E
3. A	8. B
4. B	9. C
5. C	10. D

Mapping

- Bernadete lives in a small town in Brazil, where she learns to love reading.
- Bernadete goes to boarding school in Rio de Janeiro.
- Bernadete moves to New York.
- Bernadete learns to read in English and is able to read her favorite authors again.

Answers to the Combined-Skills Tests

COMBINED SKILLS: Test 1

1. C
2. A
3. A
4. B
5. C
6. C
7. D
8. C

COMBINED SKILLS: Test 2

1. B
2. C
3. D
4. B
5. A
6. D
7. D
8. S, S, P, S

COMBINED SKILLS: Test 3

1. D
2. B
3. D
4. B
5. C
6. A
7. B
8. S, S, P, S

COMBINED SKILLS: Test 4

1. C
2. A
3. C
4. B
5. C
6. B
7. C
8. C

COMBINED SKILLS: Test 5

1. A
2. D
3. B
4. D
5. C
6. A
7. C
8. D

COMBINED SKILLS: Test 6

1. D
2. C
3. B
4. C
5. T
6. D
7. C
8. A

COMBINED SKILLS: Test 7

1. A
2. D
3. C
4. B
5. D
6. B
7. A
8. C

COMBINED SKILLS: Test 8

1. B
2. D
3. B
4. C
5. C
6. A
7. B
8. S, X, P, S

COMBINED SKILLS: Test 9

1. D
2. B
3. B
4. C
5. D
6. B
7. A
8. S, S, P, S

COMBINED SKILLS: Test 10

1. C
2. B
3. D
4. A
5. A
6. C
7. A
8. S, S, X, P

COMBINED SKILLS: Test 11

1. A
2. D
3. B
4. D
5. B
6. C
7. A
8. S, P, S, S

COMBINED SKILLS: Test 12

1. B
2. B
3. A
4. B
5. A
6. D
7. B
8. D

SUGGESTED ANSWERS TO THE DISCUSSION QUESTIONS

Note: For some questions, additional related questions have been included to enhance class discussion.

Suggested Answers to the Discussion Questions: "Phonics and Word Parts"

1   The Struggle Continues

1. Why do you think Juan's grandmother changed her mind about his going to school?

Since no one in their village had gone to school before, the whole idea of school probably seemed foreign and maybe even frightening to Juan's grandmother. She may have had a hard time understanding why Juan felt he needed school, when everyone else she knew had managed without it. Perhaps she was afraid that once he began school, he would leave her and not return. Once he did leave her, she probably realized how much he wanted an education—and once she gave her approval, Juan did return to live with her for six years, until he left for secondary school.

2. When Juan's grandmother died, Juan's mother asked him to move to the United States with her, but Juan refused her offer. What reasons might he have had for refusing her?

Answers to this question will vary. Students may suggest any or all of the following as possible reasons:

- Having not seen his mother for many years, Juan might consider her a stranger.

- Juan had successfully completed a year of secondary education in Mexico and might not have wanted to transfer to a strange American school.

- Since Juan had promised his beloved grandmother that he would continue in school (paragraph 9), perhaps he assumed she wanted him to stay in the Mexican village.

- Juan may have relied on the support of his teachers and friends in Mexico to cope with "the painful experience of losing [his] grandmother" (9).

- Juan's childhood experiences "of being mistreated by relatives" (3) may have soured him on the possibilities of a happy family life.

- Also, Juan's early experience of being "alone for most of the time" (2) and his attending school in another town have accustomed him to taking care of himself.

3. Based on the reading, what do you think are Juan's strongest personal qualities? Tell what parts of the story reveal each quality you mention.

Juan's personal characteristics include self-reliance (paragraphs 2, 3, 8, 10), industriousness (5, 10, 11), determination (3, 5, 11), good self-esteem (4, 6, 7), decisiveness (5, 8), devotion (8, 9), and optimism (11).

2   A Lesson in Love

1. *The author states that she learned of a "love that is stronger than terror." Do you think love is always stronger than terror? Or was the event the author describes just an unusual incident?*

Answers will vary.

2. *The pilot of the aircraft tells the passengers exactly what is happening, saying, for example, "we are not sure our landing gear will lock" and "we are dumping fuel from our fuel tanks. We want to have as little on board as possible in the event of a rough touchdown." Should the pilot have been so open with his passengers, who were then struck with fear, or should he have said nothing and concentrated on flying the plane? Why?*

The pilot may have needed to tell the passengers about dumping the fuel, since they were going to see the fuel spill from the tanks. Reasons in favor of the pilot's decision to speak openly are these: Passengers could prepare themselves physically and mentally for a possible crash. As in the case of the mother and little girl, loved ones could have a chance to say final words to one another. On the other hand, telling the passengers about mechanical problems they could do nothing about created enormous stress for them. In order to decide which course of action would have been wisest, students might want to put themselves in the role of the passengers.

3. *In your opinion, what is the strongest love that exists? The love of a parent for a child? What about love for a parent? Or for a spouse? Is all love the same?*

Answers will vary. Some people may say that a parent's love for a child is strongest, because the parent's role in raising that child from a helpless infant has made him or her fiercely attached to and protective of that child. The love for a parent is rooted in childhood, and has probably an element of gratitude and respect in it. The love for a spouse is more a love between two equals, since it is for a partner one has chosen as an adult.

3   Friendship and Living Longer

1. *Do you agree that "social contacts . . . provide us with a buffer against the shocks of life"? If so, what do you think are some of the ways these contacts keep us from feeling pain? Give an example.*

Some possible answers:

- In a time of "abrupt changes," as mentioned in paragraph 9, people with friends can reach out to them as a reminder that not everything has changed.
- When "the shocks of life" occur, friends comfort us by expressing concern or being there to take care of tasks we are unable to do.
- Friends can help us focus on future events, while we might brood on the past if left on our own.

2. *Why do you think playing with cats and dogs helps people in nursing homes? Is there something the animals do for patients that doctors and nurses cannot?*

Doctors and nurses provide medical care, but are not likely to have the time or inclination to provide warm, affectionate, physical contact for their patients. Nursing home residents may be embarrassed or unwilling to admit that they are lonely and in need of the comfort of touch. A dog or cat is a non-threatening source of such comfort. Pets are endlessly welcoming, friendly, and nonjudgmental in ways that may be helpful to a lonely person.

3. How can people who have trouble making friends cope with crisis? In what ways could they form social ties?

People who have difficulty making friends might seek professional help—for example, from a doctor or therapist—in a time of crisis. Counseling might also help them acquire the skills to make friends in the future. Depending on the nature of the crisis, the person might join a self-help group that brings together people struggling with similar problems.

4 From Horror to Hope

1. Was Phany's mother right in not supporting Phany's desire to continue her education by going to college? What was her mother's point of view? What was Phany's point of view? Why do you think their views were so different?

Most students will probably think Phany's mother should have been more supportive of her daughter's desire for an education. But they may also understand that under the circumstances, her mother could easily have been even less supportive. (For instance, she might have insisted that Phany take a job and pay rent to continue living at home.)

Phany's mother was raised in a culture that did not value education for girls. Undoubtedly she herself was not allowed to go to school. So it may have seemed very strange to her that this daughter of hers wanted something so foreign to her. In addition, the family was very poor. To her, higher education must have seemed like something that only rich people could hope to have. It's not surprising that she expected Phany to leave school at a young age and help to support her struggling family.

Phany, however, was thinking in a more long-term way than her mother was. Phany realized that if she left school and went to work, her life's prospects would be very narrow. If she somehow managed to continue her education, many more options would become available to her, including the option of making more money and helping her family. As someone more in touch with the modern outside world than her mother was, Phany also rebelled against the idea that girls were not worth educating.

2. What were the reasons Phany's uncle first wanted her to come to the United States? Why do you think he changed his mind and wanted to send her back to Cambodia?

Phany's uncle probably expected her to be a very traditional Cambodian girl who would accept his authority without question. He thought he would get a quiet, obedient employee and household servant for whom he would have to pay very little.

We don't know for sure why Phany's uncle decided to send her away. One possibility is this: Because the uncle seemed to care little for Phany's well-being, once he realized she was unhappy with the situation, he preferred just to get rid of her rather than to try to make her happier.

3. Phany's job at her uncle's doughnut shop turned out to be a nightmare. What is the worst job you have ever had? What made it so terrible? Describe one or two incidents that show just how awful the job was.

Answers will vary.

Suggested Answers to the Discussion Questions: "Ten Steps to College Reading"

1   A Parent Gets a Reading Lesson

1.   Why does the mother say she does not let the children have their own books at home? What effect do you think this decision has had on her children?

She says the children will tear the books up. If the children are not allowed to have books at home, they will never learn to treat books properly. They will not learn to think of books as part of normal life. It is very unlikely that they will become regular readers.

2.   What are some ways that a parent can encourage a child to love reading?

As Lucia Herndon suggests, probably the most effective way parents can encourage children to read is to read to the children when they are young and to let the children see the parents themselves reading for pleasure. Making family trips to the library is another good technique. Limiting TV, computer, and video-game time and encouraging quiet reading time works well.

3.   Educating a child is a big responsibility. Who should play a greater role—the school or the parent? Is there anything the parent can do that the school cannot?

Students' answers will probably reflect their definition of "education." If they have been raised to think of education as something that is provided at school, they will likely believe that yes, education is the school's, not the parents', job. Other students will likely point out that a parent is a child's first and most influential teacher. Endless opportunities arise for parents to educate their children, if the parents are open to such chances. They can talk about colors and numbers as they do the grocery shopping, or read street signs together, etc. Children whose parents do that sort of informal education at home have a great head start in school over children whose parents do not. In addition, parents can work one-on-one with a child, giving the child individual attention and instruction that will help the child learn; such individualization is usually impossible for teachers in a school setting. Furthermore, a parent can instill in the child a positive attitude towards education, supporting and encouraging the child to help insure that school is a good experience.

2   Discovering Words

1.   What is your impression of Malcolm X? After reading this short selection, what kind of person do you think he was?

Answers will vary, but students should mention Malcolm X's admirable qualities: his determination to learn; his willingness to copy all the words in the dictionary, no matter how slowly he wrote or how long it took, so that he could learn their meanings; and his love and respect for books. Malcolm X actually reinvented himself while in prison.

2. *At the end of the selection, Malcolm X says that even though he was still in jail, he "never had been so truly free" in his life. What does he mean by that? What is it that makes you feel free?*

Because Malcolm X now understood the meanings of so many words, the world of reading opened up to him. Because he immersed himself in reading, "months passed without [his] even thinking about being imprisoned" (paragraph 8). The act of reading mentally freed him from prison, bringing him into a world more broad than he had ever before had access to.

Answers to the second question will vary.

3. *Malcolm X decided to improve his vocabulary in order to express himself better in letters. What was it that made you decide to continue your education? What do you hope to do with the knowledge you are gaining?*

Teachers may wish to elicit varying answers and list them on the board. The benefits of an education include:

- Learning how to think better, a skill helpful in all aspects of life. (Students might be asked to name specific ways in which learning to think better is helpful.)
- Learning information helpful in viewing our relationships with the past, other people, and other countries. (Students might be asked to list specific courses that fall into this category.)
- Learning about various professions and one's own abilities and interests in order to make career decisions.
- Gaining professional background and certification.

3 One Less Sucker Lives

1. *When people on the street ask you for money, do you ever give them anything? Why or why not? If you sometimes do, how do you decide which person to help?*

Answers will vary. Many people are torn between wanting to help someone who is genuinely, temporarily down on his luck, but not wanting to help fund a person's drug or alcohol habit. Some people will give food to panhandlers, but not cash. People will have different approaches to deciding whom to help.

2. *What was the "lesson" the writer learned from the incident? If the incident had happened to you, would you feel you had learned the same lesson? Why or why not?*

The lesson the writer learned was to be less trusting and more cynical. She will be less willing to help a stranger in the future, even if he seems convincing. Students will have different answers to the second and third questions.

3. *Have you ever had to ask a stranger for help? What were the circumstances? How did the stranger respond?*

Answers will vary.

4   Classroom Notetaking

1. How would you rate yourself as a classroom notetaker? Would you give yourself an A, a B, a C, or a failing grade? Explain why.

Answers will vary, but if students are being honest, many are likely to say that they were not very good notetakers and that they had no organized style in taking notes.

Instructors might also ask, "How helpful have your notes been for reviewing material presented in class? In preparing for tests?"

2. According to the reading, part of a student's preparation for classroom notetaking should be to examine his or her attitude (paragraph 7). Why do you think the author feels examining one's attitude is so important?

Going into any situation with a good attitude is half the battle. Students who enter a classroom expecting to be bored or insisting on being entertained, or who arrive late and unprepared to listen or take notes, are almost guaranteeing that they will have a poor experience in that class. Students who go to class with a positive attitude, ready to make the best of the classroom experience, will find the class far more fulfilling.

3. Of all the advice in this selection, which three points will probably be the most helpful for you to use? Explain why.

Answers will vary.

5   Winning the Job Interview Game

1. Have you ever had a job interview? What did you learn from it?

Answers will vary.

2. If you were asked by a job interviewer, "What is your greatest weakness?" and "What is your greatest strength?" how would you answer?

Answers will vary, but remind the students of the advice given in the essay—that they might think about admitting a "weakness" that the employer might actually like, such as being a perfectionist.

3. In terms of a career, where do you see yourself in five years? How are you preparing for that goal?

Answers will vary.

6 Learning Survival Skills

1. *The author's "secrets" for survival in college and in life are "be realistic," "persist," "grow," and "enjoy." Which of these points do you feel are most important for you to remember, and why?*

Answers will vary.

2. *Jean Coleman gives a lot of advice to students just starting college. Is there anything she does not mention that you think beginning students need to know? What is it?*

Answers will vary.

3. *The author suggests that students should find out what jobs will be available in the future and then get a degree in a related field. What type of career do you think you'd be interested in, and why? What degree will help you enter that field?*

Answers will vary.

7 Migrant Child to College Woman

1. *Maria's children worked in the fields, as their mother had. In what ways are those children's lives different from Maria's life when she was a child working in the fields?*

For Maria's children, working in the fields is merely a summer job, not a way of life. They are treated kindly by their employers and parents and are not forced to do heavy work that is beyond their abilities. In addition, they keep the money they earn. Their jobs are a stepping stone to a brighter future. In Maria's case, field work seemed like all her life had to offer.

2. *Why do you think Mrs. Seth cried when she read Maria's narrative about giving phony excuses to her grade-school teacher? Why might Maria have thought that Mrs. Seth was disappointed with what she had written?*

Mrs. Seth was deeply touched to learn of the pain Maria had gone through and the courage she demonstrated by being in college. Maria's earlier experiences in school had been so negative that Maria automatically assumed the tears meant she had done poorly.

3. *What do you think Maria means when she says she encourages migrant children to "stand on their own two feet"? What do you think all children must learn in order to "stand on their own two feet"?*

For much of her own life, Maria has been a victim—of the migrant worker system, of her brutal father, of poverty, of the man who raped her. Only through tremendous personal effort and over many years has Maria learned to stand up for herself and create a better life. Maria doesn't want to see other migrant children go through the same hard process she has had to go through. By teaching them at a young age, she hopes to encourage them to be strong and independent as she now is.
    Answers to the second question will vary.

8   Life Over Death

1. *In the first paragraph, the author uses the expression "death with dignity." What do you think he means by that expression?*

   The author implies that it is wrong for "one of God's creations" to "become a permanent part of the pavement." He suggests that such a degrading end to life makes life less meaningful.

2. *Why do you think that Pokey has become, in Broderick's words, "our most beloved cat"? Do you think Pokey's injuries had an effect on how the author ended up feeling about him? Why or why not?*

   Answers will vary. One reason could be that many of us feel closest to those whom we have helped. Broderick also cannot help admiring the little cat that wanted so badly to live, sat calmly in his wife's lap and purred even though in great pain, and didn't seem to mind having his leg in a cast.

3. *Can—and—should something be done to make the world a better place for hurt and homeless animals like Pokey? Explain your answer.*

   Answers will vary, but students might consider the following:
   - Should more shelters for orphaned animals be established?
   - Should shelter animals who are not adopted be put to death (as is done at many shelters) or kept on at the shelter (as is done in some shelters)?
   - To what extent are homeless animals the result of too many dogs and cats being born?
   - Should more animals be neutered?

9   Dare to Think Big

1. *It doesn't seem likely that Dr. Carson, a highly educated adult, often uses words like "cool" and "nerd" in his own conversation. Why, then, do you think he chose to use such language in his speech at Wendell Phillips High School? What effect do you think it had on the students?*

   Dr. Carson was probably hoping to make the students realize that he was not always a successful, highly educated adult—that he was at one time a high school student like them. Like them, he was unsure of his direction in life and tempted to give up the "nerdy" habits of studying and being focused in favor of being "cool." The students were probably amused to hear Dr. Carson use such language, and they probably appreciated his efforts to speak in terms that they understood.

2. *Although Dr. Carson was a good student, he admits that peer pressure and his own hot temper sometimes got in the way of his success. What are some obstacles—internal and external—that stand in the way of your being the best student you can be? What are some ways you might overcome these obstacles?*

   Answers will vary.

3. *Dr. Carson speaks frequently to high school students because he has learned something about life that he believes can be of value to them. If you were asked to give a single piece of advice to a group of younger students, what would you say?*

   Answers will vary, but teachers may want to remind students that we can learn from our failures as well as our successes. A student's most valuable piece of advice to younger people might be to **not** repeat a mistake he or she had made.

10 Why We Shop

1. *Do you shop only for things you really need, or do you shop for other reasons? What do you think those reasons are?*

   Answers will vary, but many people shop out of habit, boredom, or as a social activity.

2. *Do you agree that shopping can be an addiction? Or do you think it is an exaggeration to say people can be "hooked" on shopping?*

   Answers will vary, but when people go deeply into debt to buy quantities of items that they do not need, they do seem to have a serious, addiction-like problem.

3. *Are advertisers to blame for encouraging people to over-shop? Are advertisers also to blame for making us place too much value on material things?*

   Answers will vary. Students might consider the enormous presence of advertising, on TV and in magazines, newspapers, billboards, buses, direct mail, etc., and how inescapable advertising is.

Suggested Answers to the Discussion Questions: Reading Selections

Note: Selections marked with an * appear only in *Groundwork for College Reading*.

1 Learning to Read: The Marvel Kretzmann Story

1. *Should Kretzmann have been "passed from grade to grade" because she was good at math? Or should she have been made to stay at a lower grade until her reading and writing skills got better?*

   Answers will vary. Students may suggest there were other alternatives (special classes, tutoring) that might have helped Kretzmann improve her reading skills and still be kept with her class.

2. *Do you know someone who has a learning disability? If so, how does that person's experience compare with Kretzmann's?*

   Answers will vary.

3. *Kretzmann says that sometimes when she is called upon to speak to small groups, she feels "uncomfortable." Why do you think this is? Would you feel uncomfortable speaking to a group? Explain.*

   Most people experience some discomfort when asked to speak in public. Being the center of attention and fearing one will do or say something foolish can be embarrassing.
   Students' answers to the question about their own experience will vary.

2 Tickets to Nowhere*

1. *What are the positive points of lotteries? What are the negatives? Everything considered, are lotteries good—or bad? Why?*

Answers will vary. Some possible positive aspects: The money raised by them goes into state-wide programs. They provide hope for people who dream of instant riches. On rare occasions, they actually make someone rich. Negative aspects: Most lottery players lose far more than they ever win. Lotteries may encourage people to pin their hopes on instant riches rather than more realistic goals. The biggest players in lotteries are usually low- or middle-income people who can't really afford what they spend.

2. *Do you know anyone like Jim, someone who depends on luck more than on hard work or ability? What do you think of this person's attitude?*

Answers will vary.

3. *If you could have a large sum of money, would it mean more to you to have earned it—or won it? Explain your answer.*

Answers will vary.

3 The Fist, the Clay, and the Rock

1. *What does Mr. Gery mean by saying that fists will come along in life? Give an example of a time you experienced a fist, or someone you know experienced a fist.*

By "fists," Mr. Gery seems to be talking about the unexpected, unpleasant events that occur in life. They might include anything: illness or an injury, the loss of a job, the death of a loved one, a romantic breakup, financial problems, etc. They are the blows in life that leave us feeling shaken and unsure of ourselves. Answers to the second question will vary.

2. *What does Mr. Gery mean by "clay"? What is the danger of being clay?*

"Clay," in Mr. Gery's illustration, seems to be a person who is shaped by whatever influence comes along. He or she is a "whatever" person, someone who goes along with the crowd, without strong convictions or a direction of his own. A "clay" person doesn't have the inner strength to survive when a blow hits him. Like a clay vase that has been dropped, a "clay" person would crumble and fall apart.

3. *What does Mr. Gery mean by "rock"? How does a person become a rock?*

By "rock," Mr. Gery is talking about a person who is strong inside. He or she sets goals and works to achieve them. While the blow of a "fist" might hurt a "rock" person, it will not destroy him or her. Rock people are strong, independent, and focused.

Mr. Gery implies that becoming a rock isn't easy; it takes time and effort. But it is possible for each of us to develop the discipline and work habits needed.

How can the adults in our lives help us become rocks?

4   A Brother's Lesson*

1. Do you think Oliver's parents were correct in their decision not to put Oliver in an institution? Why?

Answers will vary. Some students may feel that Oliver's care took too great a toll on the rest of the family, and that it would have made little difference to him if he had lived in an institution. Others may feel that a family should stay together if at all possible.

2. What was the author's first girlfriend trying to avoid by not seeing Oliver? What did it show about her as a person? What did Roe's response show about her as a person?

De Vinck's girlfriend might have been trying to avoid the sight of such a helpless adult, a person some would consider "a vegetable." Her reaction suggests that her fear of something different was greater than her compassion and love. In contrast, Roe wants to meet Oliver and soon after asks, "with ease, with freedom, with compassion" if she can feed him (paragraph 15). Her reaction indicates that she is unafraid, unselfish, compassionate, and nurturing—in short, excellently qualified to join De Vinck's family.

3. The author states that Oliver was "the weakest, most helpless human being I ever met, and yet he was one of the most powerful human beings I ever met." What do you think he means by this statement? In what ways can someone as weak and helpless as Oliver have an effect on other, stronger people?

Oliver's power resided in the effect he had on others—in particular, the other members of his family—to inspire loving and caring actions. Rather than rejecting Oliver or institutionalizing him, Oliver's parents chose to "take him home and love him" (paragraph 9). Family members had to feed and bathe Oliver, change his diapers, wash his clothes, amuse him—and in return "were blessed with his presence, a true presence of peace" (12). Oliver's existence provided opportunities for the de Vincks to give unselfishly and also reminded them of how fortunate they were to be able to live full lives (11). Indirectly, Oliver had the power to influence de Vinck's choice of a wife (16), and Oliver's memory influences de Vinck's teaching as well (2).

5   Joe Davis

1. What do you think was the main turning point in Joe's life, and why do you think it happened?

The main turning point appeared to occur as Joe lay in the hospital after his suicide attempt. Joe had reached the end of his rope. He looked realistically at his life and realized that he could choose death or life. If he continued on the same path he had been on, he would die, whether through suicide or an overdose. To live would mean to put all his energy into making the best of himself.

2. Why do you think the students Joe spoke to laughed at him as he tried to share his honest thoughts? Why did they become quieter as he continued to speak of his life? What effect do you think his presentation had on these students?

When young people are presented with something that makes them uncomfortable or embarrassed, they often laugh in an effort to seem cool and unaffected. When Joe spoke to them frankly about his experience and even the intimate physical details of his condition, their automatic reaction was laughter. If Joe had grown embarrassed or angry, they probably would have felt they had "won" and would have ignored his message. When Joe patiently continued, however, the students' respect for him seemed to grow. They overcame their own discomfort enough that they could listen. Answers to the last question will vary, but it seems likely that at least some students respected Joe's courage in coming to talk to them. They realized they were heading down the same path Joe had taken, and they questioned the wisdom of their own actions.

3. *Joe wants young people to learn the lessons he did without having to go through what he went through. What lessons have you learned in your life that you would like to pass on to others?*

Answers will vary.

6   Rosa: A Success Story

1. *As Rosa reached the border of the United States, she realized that her mother was not with her. Should she have looked for her mother, or was she right to cross into the United States when she did?*

Answers will vary. Some students may suggest that it was unwise for Rosa to leave her mother. Others may say that there was nothing Rosa could have done. Still others may say she was thinking about her brothers and had to do what was right for them. Also, some may feel that the decision must have been correct, since the family was reunited some time later.

2. *How did Rosa's education prepare her for her career? What interests and qualities would lead someone to want to work in childcare?*

Rosa first took the classes she needed to become a fluent reader and writer of English. She then concentrated on classes in early childhood education that certified her as a day-care worker. Some of the qualities needed by a person working with children include an interest in children, an understanding of their development and needs, patience, and good humor.

3. *The author writes that "we need . . . to be reminded of success stories like Rosa's." Why do you think he feels this way? What can we learn from reading Rosa's story?*

First of all, such stories remind us that the "flow of immigrants entering our country" (paragraph 21) can bring us wonderful new citizens such as Rosa and that America can be a haven for people who are oppressed. Such stories also inspire us by showing that there is tremendous opportunity in this country. If we start feeling trapped in a job or relationship, if we feel that life is closing in on us and we have nowhere to go, stories like Rosa's remind us that we can take control of our lives.

7   The Lady, or the Tiger?

1. *Do you think the tiger came out of the door, or the lady? Support your answer. If you were the princess, which door would you send your lover to?*

In support of the tiger, the story emphasized that the princess was very jealous of her lover, and that she hated the lady behind the door. In support of the lady, the princess loved the young man and certainly would not enjoy seeing him killed. Answers to the second question will vary.

2. *The princess must choose between two strong feelings: love and jealousy. In your experience, which emotion is more powerful? Explain.*

Answers will vary.

3. *In this story, the princess must make an impossible choice in a "no-win" situation. Have you ever been faced with a difficult choice in which no matter what you decided, you would be unhappy?*

Answers will vary.

8 Dawn's Story*

1. *Imagine that you were describing Dawn and her story to someone you know. What kind of person would you say Dawn is? How did she create something positive out of having survived abuse?*

Answers will vary, but most people would see Dawn as being very strong and courageous. After having been abused by many people in her life, she herself has chosen to be a loving wife and mother and to reach out to help other woman who have struggled with addiction. She has gone public with her story to help other people understand that they should not accept abuse as a necessary part of life.

2. *Have you had any direct or indirect experience with abuse? How did the abuse eventually end, if it did end? Did the abuser stop doing it, or did the person being abused find the strength to stop it?*

Answers will vary.

3. *Statistics tell us that the problem of abuse is widespread in modern society. What are some of the reasons why this might be so? What can be done to help put an end to it?*

Here are some possible reasons why people become abusive:
- They were abused themselves and have not learned better ways of dealing with their frustration or anger.
- They feel powerless in most of their lives, so they exert power by abusing those people close to them.
- They are afraid of losing their spouse or significant other, and so try to make that person feel so worthless (by abusing him or her) that he or she will not dare to leave.

For how to put an end to abuse, here are some ideas:
- Promote the idea that no one deserves to be abused, under any circumstances. Encourage victims to refuse to continue in abusive relationships.
- Teach young people skills for managing their anger, without resorting to physical violence.
- Provide special services for people who have been abused so that they can resist continuing the cycle of abuse.

9 Knowledge Is Power*

1. *The author writes that when she went to high school, students told horror stories about college. When you were in high school, what was your view of college? Now that you are in college, has your view changed? If so, in what ways?*

Answers will vary. Following are some aspects of college life that students may wish to consider:
- The amount of responsibility that students must take in college (versus the amount in high school)
- The nature of classes
- The level of difficulty of classes
- The amount of time that must be spent to get the most out of (and do well in) each class

2. *At the conclusion of the selection, the author writes that she now knows the meaning of the words "Knowledge is real power." What does that statement mean to you?*

Answers will vary. There are numerous ways in which knowledge increases our power to understand, to work, to interact, and to progress. Following are a few such ways:

- Career knowledge enhances our performance, enjoyment of work, and chances for advancement.
- Knowledge about writing improves our ability to communicate.
- Knowledge about human nature adds power to our relationships—at school, at home, at work, etc.
- Knowledge about nature gives us the power to understand scientific problems and advances in the world.

3. *The author has to work while going to school. Are you working while attending school? If so, how do you make time in your life for both responsibilities?*

Answers will vary.

10 A Love Affair with Books*

1. *The author's mother discouraged her from reading. As you were growing up, were you encouraged to read, or were you discouraged from reading? Explain why you think this was so and how it affected you.*

Answers will vary. Some ways in which young people are encouraged to read are as follows:
- Being read to from a young age onward
- Getting books as gifts
- Being taken to the library
- Seeing adults in the house read books

The absence of such encouragements can be considered discouragement. In addition, some parents, like Piassa's, may more actively discourage reading.

2. *What was reading like for you in school? Explain why it was a positive or a negative experience.*

Answers will vary. Students to whom reading was presented as an exciting, interesting activity probably found reading to be a positive experience. Those who were forced to read dull materials and materials that held little interest for them may have found reading to be a negative experience. Also, students with special reading problems that were not handled well by educators probably have many negative associations with reading in school.

3. *Are books a source of pleasure in your life? Why or why not?*

Answers will vary. Students may think of "books" as school assignments and not as a source of enjoyment. They should be reminded that there are many kinds of books . . . and that there is more than one way to read a book.

TEST BANK

This section contains the following:

- A **Test Bank** (pages 39–131) consisting of one additional Mastery Test for "Getting Started" and four additional Mastery Tests for each skills chapter in "Phonics and Word Parts" and "Ten Steps to College Reading," as well as four additional Combined-Skills Mastery Tests—57 tests in all;

- An **answer key** (pages 132–137) to the 57 tests in the test bank.

Instructors whose students are using *Groundwork for College Reading* or *Groundwork for College Reading with Phonics* in class have permission to reproduce any of these tests on a photocopying machine (or a secure website) as often as needed.

Name: _____

Section_____ Date _____

SCORE: (Number correct) × 10 = _____%

CONSONANTS: Test A

A. Complete each sentence with the word that has the hard sound of **c** (as in *can*) or of **g** (as in *game*).

1. Diana likes to add lots of *(gravy, sauce)* _____ to her dinners.

2. Kevin turned the *(corner, page)* _____.

B. Complete each sentence with the word that has the soft sound of **c** (as in *cell*) or of **g** (as in *germ*).

3. The family's pet was a *(gentle, clever)* _____ pig.

4. On Thursdays, Kenny's last class is *(English, science)* _____.

5. Janelle plays *(center, guard)* _____ on the women's basketball team.

C. In the space provided, write the letter of the answer to each question.

___ 6. In which word does the **s** sound like **z**, as in *rose*?

    A. sand   B. these   C. fast   D. slip

___ 7. Which word has a consonant blend?

    A. smile   B. choke   C. wash   D. loud

___ 8. Which word has a consonant digraph (a pair of consonants that combine to make a new sound)?

    A. tent   B. cramp   C. ghost   D. branch

___ 9. Which word has a consonant digraph sounding like **f**, as in *rough*?

    A. health   B. fling   C. photo   D. bath

___10. Which word has a silent consonant?

    A. strike   B. flame   C. hang   D. jacket

Name: _____

Section_____ Date_____

SCORE: (Number correct) × 10 = _____%

CONSONANTS: Test B

A. Answer the questions below about words in the following passage.

> [1]New York, Los Angeles, and Chicago are our nation's three largest cities. [2]All three are located near great bodies of water. [3]Both New York and Los Angeles are coastal cities, while Chicago sits on the shores of Lake Michigan. [4]All three are known by nicknames. [5]People call New York the "Big Apple." [6]Chicago is called the "Windy City" or sometimes the "Second City," while Los Angeles is known simply as "L.A."

____ 1. Which word has a soft **c** sound, as in *cell*?

    A. Chicago   B. call   C. cities   D. located

____ 2. Which word has a soft **g** sound, as in *germ*?

    A. Chicago   B. Los Angeles   C. Michigan   D. big

____ 3. Which word has a silent consonant?

    A. three   B. shores   C. simply   D. known

____ 4. Which word has a consonant digraph (a pair of consonants that combine to make a new sound)?

    A. shores   B. New York   C. Los Angeles   D. simply

____ 5. Which word has a consonant blend?

    A. shores   B. while   C. coastal   D. Chicago

B. (6–10.) Circle the five words that contain one or more consonant blends.

forehead	scratch	cereal	knee	unclean
sand	packer	retrain	playground	football

GROUNDWORK FOR
COLLEGE READING
WITH PHONICS

Name: _____

Section_____ Date _____

SCORE: (Number correct) × 10 = _____%

CONSONANTS: Test C

A. Complete each sentence with the word that has the hard sound of **c** (as in *can*) or **g** (as in *game*).

1. Some people relax by playing *(cards, gin rummy)* _____.

2. Marcus's grandmother is eighty-two, but she still likes to *(garden, dance)* _____ every chance she gets.

B. Complete each sentence with the word that has a consonant blend.

3. Tina's parents have known each other since *(college, grade school)* _____.

4. My favorite season is *(spring, fall)* _____ because the weather isn't too hot or cold then.

5. After the dog chewed up the sofa pillow, we found *(traces, pieces)* _____ of pillow everywhere.

C. Complete each sentence with the word that has a consonant digraph.

6. Tracey's favorite board game by far is *(Clue, checkers)* _____.

7. Someone once joked that you can never be too *(skinny, thin)* _____ or too rich.

8. Francisco *(chipped, broke)* _____ his tooth and had to go to the dentist.

D. Complete each sentence with the word that has a silent letter combination.

9. I always forget which side of the plate the *(knife, fork)* _____ is supposed to be on.

10. Our English teacher holds a weekly contest for the best *(writer, student)* _____ in the class.

GROUNDWORK FOR
COLLEGE READING
WITH PHONICS

Name: _____

Section_____ Date _____

SCORE: (Number correct) × 10 = _____%

CONSONANTS: Test D

A. (1–3.) Fill in each blank with the word that has a consonant blend.

¹On her days off, Carol likes to (*hunt, look*) (1)_____ through flea markets. ²Although much of what she sees is junk, she says that you would be (*surprised, shocked*) (2)_____ at some of the interesting things that people throw out. ³One day she noticed an oil painting that she found quite beautiful. ⁴She bought it for a few dollars and took it to a local art dealer to (*check, inspect*) (3)_____. ⁵He told her that it was worth five hundred dollars!

B. (4–7.) Fill in each blank with the word that has a consonant digraph.

¹Samuel was driving from Washington, D.C., to (*Philadelphia, New York*) (4)_____ for an important business meeting when it started to rain. ²At first it was a gentle (*drizzle, shower*) (5)_____, but then it fell harder. ³When it became impossible to see where he was going, Samuel had to pull the car over and wait for the rain to stop. ⁴After about (*twenty, thirty*) (6)_____ minutes, the rain stopped, but it was replaced by a thick fog. ⁵As a result of this (*rough, bad*) (7)_____ weather, Samuel was an hour and a half late for the meeting.

C. (8–10.) Fill in each blank with the word that has at least one silent letter combination.

¹Each branch of the entertainment industry has its own award ceremony to recognize the best performers and productions of the year. ²In the theater, performers are presented with an award called a Tony. ³Television awards its (*finest, most excellent*) (8)_____ performers and programs an Emmy. ⁴In music, the best songs and singers are (*picked, chosen*) (9)_____ to receive Grammy awards. ⁵A lesser-known award—the Clio—is given in advertising. ⁶Perhaps the most (*famous, well-known*) (10)_____ award is the one which is given in the motion picture industry—the Oscar.

Name: _____

Section_____ Date _____

SCORE: (Number correct) × 5 = _____%

VOWELS: Test A

Answer the questions below about words in the following passage.

> ¹People daydream for a variety of reasons. ²One cause of daydreaming is boredom, at school or on the job. ³To make life more interesting, people imagine being somewhere else. ⁴For example, a student might dream of lying on a beach and flirting with an attractive person on a nearby blanket. ⁵A factory worker might dream about winning the lottery or becoming the big boss at the company. ⁶Another cause of daydreaming is a lack of something. ⁷For instance, a starving person might dream about food, or a poor person might dream about owning a house or a car. ⁸A third cause of daydreaming is angry feelings. ⁹An angry student might dream about dropping a hated math instructor out of a classroom window.

A. Each numbered word below is from the above paragraph. Beside each word, write the sound of the boldfaced vowel:

- If the vowel is short, write ă, ĕ, ĭ, ŏ, or ŭ.
- If the vowel is long, write ā, ē, ī, ō, or ū.
- If the vowel is followed by **r**, write **r**.
- If the vowel is silent, write **silent**.

1. p**e**ople	_____	9. w**o**rker	_____
2. d**a**ydream	_____	10. b**i**g	_____
3. b**o**redom	_____	11. l**a**ck	_____
4. j**o**b	_____	12. st**a**rving	_____
5. l**i**fe	_____	13. **o**wning	_____
6. **i**nteresting	_____	14. th**i**rd	_____
7. im**a**gine	_____	15. h**a**ted	_____
8. b**ea**ch	_____		

(Continues on next page)

B. Here are the rules for long vowel sounds:

- **Silent-*e* Rule:** When a word or syllable ends in vowel-consonant-**e**, the vowel before the consonant is long and the final **e** is silent.
- **Two-Vowels-Together Rule:** When two of certain vowels are together in a word, the first vowel is long and the second is silent.
- **Final-Single-Vowel Rule:** A single vowel at the end of a word or syllable (other than a silent **e**) usually has a long sound.

Use the rules to help you place each of the following words in the correct column:

go	trace	team	float	mine

Silent-e Rule	*Two-Vowels-Together Rule*	*Final-Single-Vowel Rule*
16. _____	18. _____	20. _____
17. _____	19. _____	

Name: _____

Section_____ Date _____

SCORE: (Number correct) × 5 = _____%

VOWELS: Test B

A. In the spaces provided, write the five words in the box with short vowel sounds and the five words with long vowel sounds. When you are finished, you will have used each word below.

bite	block	clean	fill	flame
mute	punch	rag	set	slope

1. Short **a** sound: _____
2. Long **a** sound: _____
3. Short **e** sound: _____
4. Long **e** sound: _____
5. Short **i** sound: _____

6. Long **i** sound: _____
7. Short **o** sound: _____
8. Long **o** sound: _____
9. Short **u** sound: _____
10. Long **u** sound: _____

B. Here are the rules for long vowel sounds:

- **Silent-*e* Rule:** When a word or syllable ends in vowel-consonant-**e**, the vowel before the consonant is long and the final **e** is silent.
- **Two-Vowels-Together Rule:** When two of certain vowels are together in a word, the first vowel is long and the second is silent.
- **Final-Single-Vowel Rule:** A single vowel at the end of a word or syllable (other than a silent **e**) usually has a long sound.

Use the rules to help you place each of the following words in the correct column:

ago	braid	lime	load	shame

Silent-e Rule	*Two-Vowels-Together Rule*	*Final-Single-Vowel Rule*
11. _____	13. _____	15. _____
12. _____	14. _____	

C. Show whether the **oo** in each word below is long or short by checking the correct space.

	Long	*Short*
16. shoot	_____	_____
17. cookie	_____	_____
18. looking	_____	_____
19. football	_____	_____
20. moon	_____	_____

Name: _____

Section_____ Date_____

SCORE: (Number correct) × 10 = _____%

VOWELS: Test C

A. Complete each sentence with the word that has a short vowel sound. (Remember that vowels followed by an **r** are neither long nor short.)

1. Our *(pine, oak, apple)* _____ tree was damaged by lightning.

2. The little girl amused herself by playing with *(blocks, clay, paints)* _____.

3. On long business trips, Roger prefers to travel by *(car, train, jet)* _____.

B. Complete each sentence with the word that has a long vowel sound. (Remember that vowels followed by an **r** are neither long nor short.) Then, using the rules for long vowel sounds below, write the letter of the rule that the word follows.

Here are the rules for long vowel sounds:

> A **Silent-*e* Rule:** When a word or syllable ends in vowel-consonant-e, the vowel before the consonant is long and the final **e** is silent.
> B **Two-Vowels-Together Rule:** When two of certain vowels are together, the first vowel is long and the second is silent.
> C **Final-Single-Vowel Rule:** A single vowel at the end of a word or syllable (other than a silent **e**) has a long sound.

4. After sitting all day at the office, Sheila likes to go out and *(swim, jog, hike)* _____.

5. The word you chose follows this rule: _____

6. The thoroughbred is a *(breed, class, sort)* _____ of dog known for its speed.

7. The word you chose follows this rule: _____

(Continues on next page)

C. Here are the rules for **y:**

> A   In the middle of a word, **y** usually sounds like short **i.**
> B   At the end of a one-syllable word, **y** sounds like long **i.**
> C   At the end of a word with more than one syllable, **y** sounds like long **e.**

Read each sentence below, and tell which **y** rule is followed for the word indicated.

8. The history of wrestling goes back thousands of years.

   History follows this **y** rule: _____

9. It's a myth that the Great Wall of China can be seen from the moon.

   Myth follows this **y** rule: _____

10. Not all birds can fly.

   Fly follows this **y** rule: _____

GROUNDWORK FOR
COLLEGE READING
WITH PHONICS

Name: _____

Section_____ Date_____

SCORE: (Number correct) × 10 = _____%

VOWELS: Test D

Read the passages below and then answer the questions that follow.

A. [1]A recent survey asked people what they thought the biggest story of the next twenty-five years would be. [2]Some commented that it would be the end of the world. [3]Others said they believed it would be a cure for deadly diseases such as cancer. [4]Many thought that putting a colony in space would be the greatest story. [5]The number-one answer was the belief that there would be world peace.

___ 1. Which word from the paragraph has a short vowel sound?
   A. *asked*
   B. *peace*
   C. *cure*

___ 2. Which word from the paragraph has a long vowel sound that follows the two-vowels-together rule?
   A. *recent*
   B. *biggest*
   C. *peace*

___ 3. Which word from the paragraph has a long vowel sound that follows the final-single-vowel rule?
   A. *what*
   B. *they*
   C. *be*

___ 4. The word *space* is pronounced according to which rule?
   A. The silent-**e** rule
   B. The two-vowels-together rule
   C. The final-single-vowel rule

___ 5. Which word from the paragraph contains a long-**e** sound?
   A. *story*
   B. *biggest*
   C. *end*

(Continues on next page)

B. [1]Every role we play in life has an "on stage" and "backstage" area; in one we're on our best behavior, and in the other we can "let our hair down." [2]For example, in the dining room, a waiter is "on stage." [3]No matter how rushed he is or how annoyed he feels, a waiter is expected to be polite and helpful to his customers. [4]Once he returns to the kitchen, however, it's another story. [5]There he is "backstage" and can let his true feelings show. [6]In the kitchen, the waiter can make sarcastic remarks about the customers or even joke about serving a plate of food that's been dropped.

____ 6. Which word from the paragraph has a short vowel sound?
   A. *play*
   B. *rushed*
   C. *joke*

____ 7. Which word from the paragraph has a long vowel sound that follows the two-vowels-together rule?
   A. *down*
   B. *hair*
   C. *polite*

____ 8. Which word from the paragraph has a long vowel sound that follows the final-single-vowel rule?
   A. *he*
   B. *stage*
   C. *let*

____ 9. The word *make* is pronounced according to which rule?
   A. The silent-e rule
   B. The two-vowels-together rule
   C. The final-single-vowel rule

____ 10. Which word from the paragraph contains a long-**e** sound?
   A. *best*
   B. *feels*
   C. *let*

GROUNDWORK FOR
COLLEGE READING
WITH PHONICS

Name: _____

Section_____ Date_____

SCORE: (Number correct) × 10 = _____%

SYLLABLES: Test A

A. Using the rules in the box, divide the following words into syllables. For each word, also write the number of the rule that applies.

1	Divide between two consonants.
2	Divide before a single consonant.

	Syllable Division	*Rule*
1. contest	_____	_____
2. paper	_____	_____
3. water	_____	_____
4. winner	_____	_____
5. excuse	_____	_____

B. Using the rules in the box, divide the words below into syllables. For each word, also write the number of the rule that applies.

3	Divide before a consonant followed by **-le**.
4	Divide after prefixes and before suffixes.
5	Divide between the words in a compound word.

	Syllable Division	*Rule*
6. guesswork	_____	_____
7. jungle	_____	_____
8. dislike	_____	_____
9. middle	_____	_____
10. softness	_____	_____

Name: _____

Section_____ Date_____

SCORE: (Number correct) × 10 = _____%

SYLLABLES: Test B

Using the rules in the box, break the following words into syllables. Then write the numbers of the two rules that apply. For each word, first use any of rules 3–5 that apply before using rule 1 or 2.

> **1** Divide between two consonants.
> **2** Divide before a single consonant.
> **3** Divide before a consonant followed by **-le**.
> **4** Divide after prefixes and before suffixes.
> **5** Divide between the words in a compound word.

	Syllable Division	*Rules*
1. referral	_____	_____ _____
2. supporting	_____	_____ _____
3. horrible	_____	_____ _____
4. disconnect	_____	_____ _____
5. formally	_____	_____ _____
6. jellyfish	_____	_____ _____
7. innocent	_____	_____ _____
8. icebreaker	_____	_____ _____
9. successful	_____	_____ _____
10. ladylike	_____	_____ _____

Name: _____

Section_____ Date_____

SCORE: (Number correct) × 10 = _____%

SYLLABLES: Test C

Here are the rules for breaking words into syllables. Use them as you answer the questions that follow each sentence below.

> 1 Divide between two consonants.
> 2 Divide before a single consonant.
> 3 Divide before a consonant followed by **-le**.
> 4 Divide after prefixes and before suffixes.
> 5 Divide between the words in a compound word.

1. Dracula is the world's most famous vampire.

    Underline the word that follows rule 1, and divide the word here: _____

2. Even though they are good for you, Brussels sprouts are disliked by a lot of people.

    Underline the word that follows rule 2, and divide the word here: _____

3. In San Francisco, the cable cars are usually crowded with tourists.

    Underline the word that follows rule 3, and divide the word here: _____

4. In many cases, cancer is no longer treated as an incurable disease.

    Underline the word that has both a prefix and a suffix, and divide the word here:

    _____

5. That old shopping center has been vacant so long that it's become a real eyesore.

    Underline the word that follows rule 5, and divide the word here: _____

6. Many famous rock groups perform at charity concerts.

    Underline the word that follows rule 1, and divide the word here: _____

7. A certain salt mine in Poland has been in use for nearly 1,000 years.

    Underline the word that follows rule 2, and divide the word here: _____

8. If our teacher didn't mumble so much, we could understand him better.

    Underline the word that follows rule 3, and divide the word here: _____

9. High-school reunions often lead to the renewing of old friendships.

    Underline the word that has both a prefix and a suffix, and divide the word here:

    _____

10. Escape artist Harry Houdini once boasted that there were no handcuffs he couldn't get out of.

    Underline the word that follows rule 5, and divide the word here: _____

Name: _____

Section_____ Date _____

SCORE: (Number correct) × 10 = _____%

SYLLABLES: Test D

Here are the rules for breaking words into syllables. Use them as you answer the questions that follow each paragraph below.

> **1** Divide between two consonants.
> **2** Divide before a single consonant.
> **3** Divide before a consonant followed by **-le**.
> **4** Divide after prefixes and before suffixes.
> **5** Divide between the words in a compound word.

A. [1]The "Firestorm Pet Hotline" was established by pet lovers following a terrible fire in Oakland, California. [2]Here is how the Hotline works. [3]Following a disaster, volunteers take reports from people who have lost their pets. [4]Then they try to match them with reports of pets that have been found. [5]The Hotline has succeeded in reuniting hundreds of families with pets that had fled the flames of a fire or run away after an earthquake. [6]The Hotline continues its help long after a natural disaster. [7]In one case, eighteen months after a fire, a family was reunited with its dog that had been found eight miles away. [8]Two months after that, a stray cat was reunited with its family.

1. Underline the word from sentence 8 that follows rule 1, and divide the word here:

   _____

2. Underline the two-syllable word from sentence 3 that follows rule 2, and divide the word here: _____

3. Underline the word from sentence 3 that follows rule 3, and divide the word here:

   _____

4. Underline the word from sentence 5 that has both a prefix and a suffix, and divide the word here: _____

5. Underline one of the three words from sentence 1 that follows rule 5, and divide the word here: _____

(Continues on next page)

B. [1]If you wear eyeglasses, you may wonder what to do with a pair that is old-fashioned or no longer right for your eyes. [2]Don't throw them away—someone else may be able to use them. [3]Lions Club International, a service organization found throughout the country, has set up recycling centers for unneeded glasses. [4]Once the eyeglasses are collected, they are arranged according to prescription and type. [5]They are then cleaned and made available to the 500 million people around the world who need glasses but cannot afford them.

6. Underline the two-syllable word from sentence 4 that follows rule 1, and divide the word here: _____

7. Underline the two-syllable word from sentence 2 that follows rule 2, and divide the word here: _____

8. Underline the word from sentence 2 that follows rule 3, and divide the word here:

_____

9. Underline the word from sentence 4 that has both a prefix and a suffix, and divide the word here: _____

10. Underline the word from sentence 3 that follows rule 5, and divide the word here:

_____

Name: _____

Section_____ Date _____

SCORE: (Number correct) × 10 = _____%

WORD PARTS: Test A

Use the word parts in the box to complete the words in the sentences below. Use each word part only once.

er (or)—a person who does something	**mis**—badly; wrong
ful—full of	**pre**—before
ish—similar to	**re**—again; back
ly—in a certain way; at a certain time	**super**—over; above; beyond
man (manu)—hand	**ven (vent)**—come

1. As a precaution against terrorism, all airline passengers must now *(. . .move)* _____ their shoes before boarding a flight.

2. Because my *(. . .visor)* _____ is very demanding, I always double-check my work before handing it to her.

3. Some *(elder. . .)* _____ people find great pleasure in tutoring youngsters.

4. Jeannie *(. . .behaved)* _____ by sneaking into the kitchen and stuffing herself with cookies when her parents left her with a babysitter.

5. For some reason, my *(plumb. . .)* _____ made fun of the idea that clogged drains can be treated with store-bought chemicals.

6. A trainer has to be both patient and *(force. . .)* _____ when getting problem dogs to obey commands.

7. I felt *(sheep. . .)* _____ when I looked down at my feet and saw that I had worn my bedroom slippers to work.

8. We were excited to learn that we could earn money simply by *(. . .viewing)* _____ upcoming TV shows.

9. Shameka wasn't sure she wanted to become *(. . .ager)* _____ of the Bon Ton Shop because she knew that it would mean working longer hours.

10. The *(in. . .tion)* _____ of air conditioning made living in the South and Southwest more attractive to many Americans.

**GROUNDWORK FOR
COLLEGE READING
WITH PHONICS**

Name: _____

Section_____ Date _____

SCORE: (Number correct) × 10 = _____%

WORD PARTS: Test B

Use the word parts in the box to complete the words in the sentences below. Use each word part only once.

able (ible)—able to be	**ment**—state of being
aud (audi, audit)—hear	**post**—after
auto—self	**pre**—before
ist—a person skilled at something	**spect**—look
ly—in a certain way; at a certain time	**tele**—far; over a distance

1. If you're waiting for an important call, the last thing you want to hear is the voice of a *(. . .marketer)* _____ when you pick up the phone.

2. After World War II ended in 1946, so many Americans started families in the *(. . .war)* _____ years of 1946–1960 that our nation experienced a "baby boom."

3. Everyone told Carmen that she should *(. . .tion)* _____ for a part in the school musical, since she has such a beautiful singing voice.

4. My little brother Teddy loves to throw his *(inflat. . .)* _____ toys into the swimming pool.

5. In the early 1900s, the United States government passed a law that provided for federal *(in. . .ion)* _____ of meat products.

6. As strange as it may seem, the ruins of ancient castles are often quite *(love. . .)* _____.

7. As *(punish. . .)* _____ for egging a neighbor's front door, Albert's dad made him wash the mess off the door and grounded him for a month.

8. My friends joke that I look like I'm on *(. . .pilot)* _____ when I'm daydreaming.

9. Because he considers himself a *(conservation. . .)* _____, Jeremy bought a compact car that gets excellent gas mileage.

10. Before the invention of the refrigerator, many farm women used to *(. . .serve)* _____ fruits and vegetables in Mason jars.

Name: _____

Section_____ Date_____

SCORE: (Number correct) × 10 = _____%

WORD PARTS: Test C

A. Use the word parts in the box to complete the words in the sentences below. Use each word part only once.

bene—good, well	**mono**—one
bio—life	**re**—again; back
in (im)—within, into; not	

1. After his rent was raised $100 a month, Mr. Bellamy decided to *(. . .locate)* _____ his music shop to a nearby town.

2. Don't bother to try having a conversation with my Aunt Elsa. She's so talkative that she might as well be delivering a *(. . .logue)* _____.

3. When the fog rolls in over San Francisco, even the Golden Gate Bridge becomes so *(. . .distinct)* _____ that you can barely see it.

4. President Richard Nixon signed an order in November, 1969, which stopped production of *(. . .logical)* _____ weapons in the U.S.

5. A great *(. . .fit)* _____ of working from home is that you can't get caught in rush-hour traffic.

B. Use the word parts in the box to complete the words in the following passage. Read the passage through one time before trying to complete the words. Use each word part once.

in (im)—within, into; not	**port**—carry
less—without	**un**—not
ment—state of being	

[1]Have you noticed that sometimes the most *(. . .likely)* (6)_____ pairs form the best friendships? [2]In late December 2004, flood waters washed a baby hippo's entire family out to sea, leaving him stranded in the rough waters along the coast of Kenya in East Africa. [3]Local people rescued the struggling hippo from the ocean and named him Owen. [4]Then they *(trans. . .ed)* (7)_____ Owen several miles away to Haller Wildlife Park, which serves as a wildlife orphanage. [5]To everyone's *(astonish. . .)* (8)_____, Owen trotted right up to a giant gray tortoise. [6]At first the tortoise hissed at Owen, but by the next morning the two were *(. . .separable)* (9)_____. [7]It seems that Owen was *(mother. . .)* (10)_____ no longer. [8]He had "adopted" the tortoise as his parent.

Name: _____

Section_____ Date_____

SCORE: (Number correct) × 10 = _____%

WORD PARTS: Test D

Use the word parts in the box to complete the words in the sentences below. Use each word part only once.

aud (audi, audit)—hear	**mis**—badly; wrong
ex—out; from	**ped (pod)**—foot
ful—full of	**sub**—below; under
ism—a practice; a belief or set of principles	**un**—not
ist—a person skilled at something	**ven (vent)**—come

1. To keep track of how far he runs, Kenyon wears a *(. . .ometer)* _____ clipped to his belt.

2. I wish our geometry teacher would stop mumbling; as it is now, he's barely *(. . .ible)* _____.

3. We were saddened when the old Miller farm was sold and *(. . .divided)* _____ into much smaller properties.

4. My car developed engine trouble just two days after its warranty *(. . . pired)* _____.

5. Christians who practice *(fundamental. . .)* _____ believe that the world was created in six days, as it states in the Bible.

6. Although Helen Keller was blind and deaf, she learned how to talk with the help of a speech *(therap. . .)* _____.

7. Unless you're expecting a refund, income tax time can be rather *(stress. . .)* _____.

8. Commercials for weight-loss products are often *(. . .leading)* _____. They claim that people can lose weight almost overnight and with very little effort.

9. Francisco and Carla were *(. . .decided)* _____ about where to go on their vacation, but they finally settled on taking a cruise to Bermuda.

10. Job titles sometimes change. A few years ago, our store had employees who worked in "Security," but now their title is "Loss *(Pre. . .tion)* _____."

Name: _____

Section_____ Date_____

SCORE: (Number correct) × 10 = _____%

GETTING STARTED: Test

In the space provided, answer each of the questions below.

____ 1. When you regularly attend class, you will
   A. learn material that is not contained in any textbook.
   B. realize that it is not necessary to read your textbook.
   C. learn which ideas the instructor feels are most important.
   D. probably receive an A in the course.

____ 2. Studies have shown that the amount of class material forgotten in two weeks is
   A. 20 percent.
   B. 40 percent.
   C. 60 percent.
   D. 80 percent.

____ 3. The percentage of class material that people typically forget within four weeks is
   A. 75 percent.
   B. 80 percent.
   C. 90 percent.
   D. 95 percent.

____ 4. A syllabus is a
   A. large monthly calendar.
   B. course outline.
   C. "to do" list.
   D. written record of what an instructor presents in class.

____ 5. Your large monthly calendar should include
   A. a list of items that need to be done each day.
   B. starting and ending times for all your courses.
   C. the dates of exams and when papers or reports are due.
   D. all of the above.

____ 6. Keeping a "to do" list will help you to
   A. keep track of your daily expenses.
   B. decide which items are most important and handle them first.
   C. compare your progress with that of your friends.
   D. study your textbooks every day.

(Continues on next page)

_____ 7. When a panel of first-year college students were asked to give advice to high school students, they advised them to
   A. develop a winning attitude.
   B. read everything they could.
   C. pay better attention in class.
   D. practice note-taking.

_____ 8. Ben Carson developed the reading habit and went on to become
   A. a well-respected writer.
   B. the president of Johns Hopkins University Hospital.
   C. a skilled chef.
   D. a world-famous neurosurgeon.

_____ 9. Author John Langan compares doing a lot of reading to
   A. studying cookbooks.
   B. taking a class on how to cook.
   C. helping out a good cook.
   D. practicing cooking.

_____ 10. Langan challenges students to
   A. read at least one outside book at the same time they are using *Groundwork for College Reading*.
   B. speed up the rate at which they read.
   C. buy the book *Reading Changed My Life!* and write a book report about it.
   D. all of the above.

Name: _____

Section_____ Date _____

SCORE: (Number correct) × 5 = _____%

DICTIONARY USE: Test A

A. Below are five pairs of dictionary guidewords followed by a series of other words. Circle the two words in each series which would be found on the page with the guidewords.

1–2. **broken-down / brown**

broil   brunch   bronze   bug   brother

3–4. **crutch / cueball**

crude   Cupid   crystal   crumble   cucumber

5–6. **haystack / headquarters**

heartless   headlight   haze   haunt   headstand

7–8. **robotics / role**

roadway   romance   rocky   robe   rodeo

9–10. **whirlpool / whitewash**

whiz   whig   whitefish   whole   whisper

B. Use your dictionary and the spelling hints in the textbook to find the correct spelling of the following words.

11. peice _____   14. invenshun _____

12. reveel _____   15. dissapear _____

13. trajedy _____   16. ekwipmint _____

C. Use the pronunciation key below to answer the following questions.

ă hat	ā pay	âr care	ä card	ĕ ten	ē she	ĭ sit
ī hi	îr here	ŏ lot	ō go	ô all	oi oil	ou out
o͝o look	yo͝o cure	o͞o cool	yo͞o use	ŭ up	ûr fur	th thick
th then	ə ago, item, easily, gallop, circus					

17. The **i** in *primary* (prī′mər′ē) is pronounced like the **i** in what common word?

_____

18. The first **e** in *defend* (dĭ-fĕnd′) is pronounced like the **i** in what common word?

_____

19. The **o** in *slope* (slōp) is pronounced like the **o** in what common word? _____

20. The **a** in *tattoo* (tă-to͞o′) is pronounced like the **a** in what common word?

_____

Name: _____

Section_____ Date _____

SCORE: (Number correct) × 5 = _____%

DICTIONARY USE: Test B

Use your dictionary as needed to answer the questions below.

A. Place dots between the syllables in the following words. Then write the correct pronunciation symbols, including the accent marks. Use the pronunciation key below.

1. s u s p e c t _____
4. a r m c h a i r _____

2. g i v e n _____
5. b r a i n s t o r m _____

3. m o s t l y _____
6. w a s h b o w l _____

B. List the parts of speech for the following words. Each word has more than one part of speech.

7. care _____
9. rent _____

8. slow _____
10. which _____

C. Write the plural form for each of the following words.

11. leaf _____
13. gypsy _____

12. hero _____
14. cactus _____

D. Use the following pronunciation key, if necessary, to answer the questions about the four words below.

A. **blue•bird** (blo͞o′bûrd′)
C. **i•o•ta** (ī-ō′tə)

B. **ham•mer•head** (hăm′ər-hĕd′)
D. **sting** (stĭng)

ă hat	ā pay	âr care	ä card	ĕ ten	ē she	ĭ sit
ī hi	îr here	ŏ lot	ō go	ô all	oi oil	ou out
o͝o look	yo͝o cure	o͞o cool	yo͞o use	ŭ up	ûr fur	th thick
th then	ə ago, item, easily, gallop, circus					

15. Which word has the sound of **a** as in *hat*? _____

16. Which word has the sound of **i** as in *sit*? _____

17. Which two words have a schwa sound?

_____   _____

18. Which two words have both a stronger and a weaker accent?

_____   _____

19. Which word has two long vowel sounds? _____

20. Which word has only one syllable? _____

DICTIONARY USE: Test C

A. Below are three pairs of dictionary guidewords followed by other words. Circle the two words in each series which would be found on the page with the guidewords.

1–2. clutter / coax

cobbler   coaster   cobweb   coachman   cluster

3–4. guidebook / gumbo

gull   guff   guard   guilt   gunfight

5–6. mute / mystery

muzzle   mustard   myrtle   myth   musty

B. Answer the questions below about the following partial dictionary entry for *liberal*.

lib•er•al (lib′ər-əl) *adj.* **1.** Open-minded; tolerant. **2.** Generous. **3.** Not strict. **4.** Based on the traditional arts and sciences of a college or university curriculum: *a liberal education.* —*n.* A person with liberal ideas or opinions.

____ 7. The parts of speech of *liberal* are
   A. verb and adjective.
   B. noun and verb.
   C. adjective and noun.

____ 8. *Liberal* has
   A. one syllable.
   B. two syllables.
   C. three syllables.

____ 9. The definition of *liberal* that fits the sentence below is
   A. definition 1.
   B. definition 2.
   C. definition 3.
   D. definition 4.

   Our boss gave a very liberal donation to the United Fund.

____ 10. The definition of *liberal* that fits the sentence below is
   A. definition 1.
   B. definition 2.
   C. definition 3.
   D. definition 4.

   My liberal parents have always been open to new and differing ideas.

(Continues on next page)

C. Use your dictionary and the spelling hints in the textbook to find the correct spelling of the following words.

11. hevvy _____   14. aufull _____

12. jin rumy _____   15. totel _____

13. offishal _____   16. casheer _____

D. Use the pronunciation key below to answer the following questions.

ă hat	ā pay	âr care	ä card	ĕ ten	ē she	ĭ sit
ī hi	îr here	ŏ lot	ō go	ô all	oi oil	ou out
ŏŏ look	yŏŏ cure	ōō cool	yōō use	ŭ up	ûr fur	th thick
th then	ə ago, item, easily, gallop, circus					

17. In *fellow* (fĕl′ō), the **e** is pronounced like the e in what common word?

    _____

18. In *fellow* (fĕl′ō), the **o** is pronounced like the o in what common word?

    _____

19. In *wizard* (wĭz′ərd), the **i** is pronounced like the i in what common word?

    _____

20. In *wizard* (wĭz′ərd), the **a** is pronounced like the a in what common word?

    _____

DICTIONARY USE: Test D

Use your dictionary as needed to answer the questions below.

A. Put dots between the syllables in each word. Then write out the word with the correct pronunciation symbols, including accent marks.

1. b e v e r a g e _____

2. e i g h t i e t h _____

3. p o i s o n _____

4. m a n h a n d l e _____

5. s y m p h o n y _____

B. List the parts of speech for the following words. Each word has more than one part of speech.

6. bar _____

7. fashion _____

8. mother _____

C. Write the irregular forms provided in the dictionary entries for the following words.

9. many _____

10. swim _____

11. sentry _____

12. break _____

D. Use your dictionary to answer the following questions.

____ 13. If water is *potable*, it
    A. is polluted.
    B. is safe to drink.
    C. must be boiled before it can be drunk.
    D. has been mixed with another liquid.

____ 14. A *minuteman*
    A. focuses on details that others often miss.
    B. was a soldier during the American Civil War.
    C. is another name for a fast-food cook.
    D. fought during the American Revolutionary War.

____ 15. If something is *combustible*, it is
    A. fireproof.
    B. likely to catch fire and burn.
    C. waterproof.
    D. very heavy.

(Continues on next page)

E. Use the following pronunciation key, if necessary, to answer the questions about the four words below.

A. **dec•o•rate** (dĕk′ə-rāt′) C. **o•ver•blown** (ō′vər-blōn′)

B. **pro•gres•sive** (prə-grĕs′ĭv) D. **pil•low** (pĭl′ō)

ă hat	ā pay	âr care	ä card	ě ten	ē she	ĭ sit
ī hi	îr here	ŏ lot	ō go	ô all	oi oil	ou out
ŏŏ look	yŏŏ cure	ōō cool	yōō use	ŭ up	ûr fur	th thick
th then	ə ago, item, easily, gallop, circus					

16. Which two words have the sound of **o** as in *go*?

_____

17. Which two words have the sound of **i** as in *sit*?

_____

18. Which three words have a schwa sound?

_____

19. Which two words have both a stronger and a weaker accent?

_____

20. Which word has only two syllables?

_____

VOCABULARY IN CONTEXT: Test A

A. Read each item below and then do two things:

    1 Underline the **examples** that suggest the meaning of the word in italics.

    2 In the space provided, write the letter of the meaning of the word in italics.

___ 1. Milo told his blind date to wear something *conspicuous*, such as a bright red dress, a rose in her hair, or a big hat.

    Conspicuous means

    A. very expensive.   B. serious.   C. noticeable.

___ 2. When Jackie Robinson became the first African American to play major league baseball, some white fans became *hostile*. They shouted insults at him and even threatened his life.

    Hostile means

    A. proud.   B. very unfriendly.   C. interested.

B. In each item, underline the **synonym** for the word in italics. The synonym may be one or more words.

    3. Dave's English class was watching an *excerpt* from the movie version of *Romeo and Juliet*. It was the part where the two young lovers meet at a party.

    4. Can you *recollect* anything from when you were two or three years old? Most people cannot remember anything from those years.

    5. The deep love people share when they get married can become even more *profound* as they share the joys of having children and growing as a family.

C. Antonyms provide context clues in the sentences below. Read each item and do two things:

    1 Underline the **antonym** for the word in italics. Each antonym may be one or more words.

    2 In the space provided, write the letter of the meaning of the word in italics.

___ 6. If the fifth-grade teacher sees an *idle* student, she makes sure he's soon busy.

    Idle means

    A. active.   B. early.   C. not busy.

___ 7. People used to think of Japanese electronics as *inferior to* American products. Now many believe that they're the best available.

    Inferior to means

    A. lower in quality or value than.   B. related to.   C. better than.

(Continues on next page)

D. Use the **general sense of each sentence** to figure out the meaning of each word in italics. Then write the letter of the meaning of the word in italics.

_____ 8. The audience members asked themselves, "How much longer must we *endure* this boring talk?"

Endure means

    A. enjoy.   B. put up with.   C. finish.

_____ 9. When it comes to flying saucers, most scientists are *skeptics*—they question why no spaceships have ever landed in public places.

Skeptics means

    A. supporters.   B. doubters.   C. victims.

_____10. When the rock hit the moon's reflection in the pool, many tiny pieces of silver light *dispersed* throughout the water.

Dispersed means

    A. scattered.   B. sank.   C. held back.

VOCABULARY IN CONTEXT: Test B

Using context clues for help, write the letter of the meaning of each word in italics.

____ 1. You are required to *disclose* all your earnings to the Internal Revenue Service.

Disclose means

A. plan.　　　　　B. make known.　　　　　C. remove.

____ 2. It may be hard for Sandra to *adapt* to living in Maine. She's used to the hot, sunny climate of Atlanta, Georgia.

Adapt means

A. adjust.　　　　　B. survive.　　　　　C. live.

____ 3. When Ben first started working in customer service, it was difficult for him to remain calm when dealing with *irate* customers.

Irate means

A. pleasant.　　　　　B. angry.　　　　　C. serious.

____ 4. Flooding forced us to leave our house. We were allowed to return the next day, when the flood waters had *receded* enough.

Receded means

A. risen.　　　　　B. reappeared.　　　　　C. moved back.

____ 5. When I was sick with the flu, my favorite spicy foods looked awful to me; all I wanted was *bland* foods such as broth and toast.

Bland means

A. fattening.　　　　　B. dull.　　　　　C. expensive.

____ 6. Although ballerinas look thin and weak, the *rigorous* training they undergo would probably challenge a pro football player.

Rigorous means

A. easy.　　　　　B. meaningless.　　　　　C. strict.

____ 7. Would you believe that the itch between your shoulder blades could be *genetic*? Well, it's true—certain itchy spots can be passed on from parent to child.

Genetic means

A. imaginary.　　　　　B. inherited.　　　　　C. unimportant.

____ 8. I had always *assumed* that my cousin Leo and his wife were happily married, so I was shocked to hear they were getting a divorce.

Assumed means

A. refused to believe.　　　　　B. believed to be true.　　　　　C. complained.

(Continues on next page)

____ 9. Deer were thought to be vegetarians until two biologists *observed* some white-tailed deer gulping down hundreds of tiny fish that had washed up on a beach.

Observed means

A. ignored.　　　　　B. imagined.　　　　　C. saw.

____10. We don't always know if a college course we're taking will help us later in life. Sometimes it's hard to *evaluate* a course until we're out of school.

Evaluate means

A. judge the value of.　　B. influence the value of.　　c. ignore the value of.

VOCABULARY IN CONTEXT: Test C

Using context clues for help, write the letter of the meaning of each word in italics.

____ 1. The townspeople feared that *toxic* run-off from the paint factory would be a danger to their community.

Toxic means

    A. strong.   B. poisonous.   C. harmless.

____ 2. No one is sure how much the threat of execution *deters* murder.

Deters means

    A. encourages.   B. causes.   C. discourages.

____ 3. Terri's *objective* is to become a world-famous author; her sister Susan's goal is to get married and have three or four healthy children.

An *objective* is a

    A. relationship.   B. goal.   C. complaint.

____ 4. Most people prefer to *isolate* themselves when they meditate, but Michi can meditate anywhere, even on a bus.

Isolate means

    A. enjoy.   B. separate from others.   C. delay.

____ 5. Our cat hates going to the vet, so we have to *lure* her into her carrier by placing a bowl of tuna inside.

Lure means

    A. see.   B. imitate.   C. attract.

____ 6. His parents were relieved to see Nate change from an *obnoxious* teenager into a kind, thoughtful young man.

Obnoxious means

    A. cheerful.   B. very unpleasant.   C. simple.

____ 7. The criminal managed to *evade* capture for years by hiding in a cabin deep in the Smoky Mountains.

Evade means

    A. escape.   B. expect.   C. face.

____ 8. The *concept* of saving some of his earnings seems to have never crossed Roland's mind. His favorite saying is, "Money is for spending."

Concept means

    A. explanation.   B. idea.   C. habit.

(Continues on next page)

_____ 9. It's hard to get a sense of how *vast* the Grand Canyon is without seeing it in person. When you're there, it seems to go on and on as far as the eye can see.

Vast means

A. old.   B. limitless.   C. beautiful.

_____10. Tomato plants tend to *thrive* in hot, sunny climates, but do poorly if the weather gets too chilly.

Thrive means

A. grow well.   B. stay the same.   C. suffer.

VOCABULARY IN CONTEXT: Test D

A. Using context clues for help, write the letter of the meaning of each word in italics.

____ 1. My grandfather was an energetic man until he died at 91. He felt one reason for his *vigor* was the raw garlic clove he ate every day.

Vigor means

A. taste.   B. energy.   C. death.

____ 2. A person who is born with an *innate* talent for something, such as music or art, must still work to become skilled in that field.

Innate means

A. missing.   B. harmful.   C. natural.

____ 3. A donut and a diet soda is no one's idea of an *adequate* breakfast. Rather, granola and milk, or fruit and yogurt, would be better selections.

Adequate means

A. delicious.   B. simple.   C. good enough.

____ 4. As Paula walked to the bus stop in the biting wind, she began to wish that she had worn her winter coat rather than a *flimsy* jacket.

Flimsy means

A. light and thin.   B. sturdy.   C. colorful.

____ 5. One way to *stimulate* children's imagination is to provide them with art supplies such as colored paper, crayons, and glue.

Stimulate means

A. recognize.   B. make active.   C. delay.

(Continues on next page)

B. Read both paragraphs below. Then, using context clues for help, write the letter of the meaning of each word in italics.

[1]Scientists have long wondered why heart disease is the leading cause of death in most industrialized countries, but not in France. [2]Some researchers *investigated* the eating and drinking habits of people in industrialized countries. [3]They found that the French eat foods with as much cholesterol as the foods people in other countries eat. [4]Cholesterol is thought to be a *principal* cause of heart disease. [5]Therefore, general diet was *eliminated* as the reason for the French having less heart disease.

[6]Other studies looked at people's drinking habits. [7]They found a difference in what the French and others drank with their meals. [8]While people in other countries drank water, milk, beer, and white wines, the French *imbibed* red wine. [9]There is a chemical in red wine that *diminishes* cholesterol levels. [10]Thus, it may be that the French suffer less heart disease because they drink red wine.

____ 6. *Investigated* means

    A. ignored.   B. studied.   C. enjoyed.

____ 7. *Principal* means

    A. main.   B. worthless.   C. useful.

____ 8. *Eliminated* means

    A. accepted.   B. rejected.   C. added.

____ 9. *Imbibed* means

    A. produced.   B. drank.   C. disliked.

____ 10. *Diminishes* means

    A. lowers.   B. makes.   C. arranges.

Name: _____

Section_____ Date_____

SCORE: (Number correct) × 4 = _____%

MAIN IDEAS: Test A

A. Each group of words below consists of one general idea and four specific ideas. The general idea includes all the specific ideas. Underline the general idea in each group.

1. wife   grandfather   relative   mother-in-law   uncle

2. oval   shape   circle   diamond   square

3. marvelous   great   outstanding   compliment   lovely

4. Oscar   Emmy   first prize   Nobel Prize   award

5. fingerprints   hairs   clues   bloodstains   ransom notes

B. In each item below, one idea is general and one is specific. In the spaces provided, write two more specific ideas that are covered by the general idea.

6–7. *General idea:* meal
Specific ideas: breakfast, _____, _____

8–9. *General idea:* dog
Specific ideas: cocker spaniel, _____, _____

10–11. *General idea:* holiday
Specific ideas: Valentine's Day, _____, _____

12–13. *General idea:* appliance
Specific ideas: washing machine, _____, _____

14–15. *General idea:* metal
Specific ideas: gold, _____, _____

C. In each pair below, one idea is general and the other is specific. The general idea includes the specific idea. Do two things:

1 Underline the general idea in each pair.
2 Write in one more specific idea that is covered by the general idea.

16–17. rock 'n' roll   music   _____

18–19. athlete   Tiger Woods   _____

20–21. wild animal   gorilla   _____

22–23. coin   dime   _____

24–25. pretzel   snack   _____

MAIN IDEAS: Test B

A. Each group of words below consists of one general idea and four specific ideas. The general idea includes all the specific ideas. Underline the general idea in each group.

    1. bus   airplane   bicycle   vehicle   automobile

    2. golf   tennis   needlepoint   taking a nap   leisure activity

    3. trombone   piano   musical instrument   guitar   drums

    4. biology   science   physics   astronomy   zoology

    5. salmon   flounder   cod   fish   tuna

B. In each item below, one idea is general and one is specific. In the spaces provided, write two more specific ideas that are covered by the general idea.

    6–7. *General idea:* reply
          Specific ideas: "no,"   _____,   _____

    8–9. *General idea:* dessert
          Specific ideas: apple pie,   _____,   _____

  10–11. *General idea:* outdoor job
          Specific ideas: lawn mowing,   _____,   _____

  12–13. *General idea:* school subject
          Specific ideas: English,   _____,   _____

C. In each pair below, one idea is general and the other is specific. The general idea includes the specific idea. Do two things:

    1 Underline the general idea in each pair.
    2 Write in one more specific idea that is covered by the general idea.

  14–15. farm animal   pig   _____

  16–17. heart   organ   _____

  18–19. drink   beer   _____

(Continues on next page)

D. In the space provided, write the letter of the topic of the paragraph below. Make sure your choice is not too general or too specific.

[1]The word "pet" has an interesting history. [2]Some believe that it came from the French word "petit," meaning "little." [3]First applied to people, "pet" was used by the early 1500s to describe a child who was treated as a favorite. [4]By the mid-sixteenth century, "pets" included animals that were tamed and kept for pleasure or companionship. [5]The term was especially applied to orphan lambs that required raising by hand. [6]Nowadays, it can be applied to anything from a cat to a hamster to a horse.

___ 20. The topic is

    A. favorite pets.

    B. the word "pet."

    C. types of animals.

Name: _____

Section_____ Date _____

SCORE: (Number correct) × 20 = _____%

MAIN IDEAS: Test C

In the space provided, write the letter of the topic of each paragraph below. Make sure your choice is not too general or too specific.

____ 1. [1]Water is essential to the human body. [2]We can go weeks without food, but only two or three days without water. [3]Water is needed for the body to wash away its waste products. [4]It also moistens the body's tissues so they can carry oxygen.

The topic is

A. the human body.

B. water and the human body.

C. food and the human body.

____ 2. [1]For centuries, the best treatment for tuberculosis (TB), a dangerous lung disease, was fresh air, rest, and exercise. [2]Then in 1944, researchers discovered an antibiotic that was effective against the disease. [3]Until the mid-1980s, tuberculosis seemed to be fading away. [4]But today TB is back again and deadlier than ever. [5]It is affecting people with AIDS. [6]Residents of crowded environments such as homeless shelters are catching it too. [7]The tuberculosis that people are catching today resists antibiotics.

The topic is

A. TB in the mid-1980s.

B. disease.

C. tuberculosis.

____ 3. [1]Do you feel safer driving in an automobile or flying on a commercial airplane? [2]If you are like most people, the flight feels riskier than the drive to the airport. [3]However, statistics indicate that each time you fly on a U.S. commercial aircraft, your chances of arriving without a fatal accident are better than 10 million to 1. [4]In contrast, according to the National Safety Council, 1 out of every 5,000 automobiles in the United States is involved in a fatal accident every year.

The topic is

A. automobile accidents.

B. safe airlines.

C. airline safety compared to auto safety.

(Continues on next page)

____ 4. [1]Attitudes toward alcohol use vary from group to group. [2]For instance, in the United States, Jewish-, Italian-, Greek-, and Chinese-Americans have a tradition of moderate drinking. [3]Drinking alcohol may be limited to particular social occasions, such as weddings and other formal celebrations. [4]Some U.S. religious groups, such as Mormons, Amish, and Muslims, forbid drinking under any circumstances. [5]Asian-Americans and African-Americans have the lowest rates of alcohol use.

The topic is

A. U.S. religious groups.
B. differing attitudes toward alcohol.
C. formal celebrations in America.

____ 5. [1]Because you are always the "author" of your dreams, it is not surprising that you often play a leading role. [2]The dreamer has an active role in nearly three-fourths of dreams, and you are absent from your own dreams only 10 percent of the time. [3]About half of the other characters in your dreams are people you recognize, but the other half are people you do not know or cannot recognize—or, 4 percent of the time, are animals. [4]The characters in dreams are about an equal mixture of men and women, with men being slightly more likely to dream about men than women are.

The topic is

A. dreams.
B. characters in dreams.
C. how men and women dream.

MAIN IDEAS: Test D

In the space provided, write the letter of the topic of each of the following paragraphs. Then find the sentence that states the main idea about the topic, and write the letter of that sentence.

[1]One theory used to describe the business of advertising is called the A-T-R theory. [2]According to the A-T-R theory, there are three stages in the selling process: Awareness, Trial, and Reinforcement. [3]Awareness of a product is achieved through advertising. [4]To bring about the trial stage, many companies give away free samples or coupons. [5]Reinforcement involves constantly reminding the consumer to try the product again.

____ 1. The topic is
   A. A-T-R and the awareness of a product.   C. business.
   B. the A-T-R theory.

____ 2. The main idea is stated in sentence
   A. 1.   B. 2.   C. 5.

[1]Every role we play in life has an "on stage" and "backstage" area; in one we're on our best behavior, and in the other we can "let our hair down." [2]For example, in the dining room, a waiter is "on stage." [3]No matter how rushed he is or how annoyed he feels, a waiter is expected to be polite and helpful to his customers. [4]Once he returns to the kitchen, however, it's another matter. [5]There he is "backstage" and can let his true feelings show. [6]In the kitchen, the waiter can make sarcastic remarks about the customers or even joke about serving a plate of food that's been dropped.

____ 3. The topic is
   A. human behavior of waiters.   C. "backstage" roles.
   B. "on stage" and "backstage" roles.

____ 4. The main idea is stated in sentence
   A. 1.   B. 2.   C. 5.

[1]When you're hiking, and you're still miles from your campsite, a bandanna (a large handkerchief often used as a head scarf) can be used as a headband to keep hair and sweat out of your eyes. [2]In fact, the bandanna is one of the most useful "tools" you can bring on a camping trip. [3]You can also wear one "bandit-style" to protect your face from the cold. [4]And around the campfire, you can use bandannas as potholders and for washing and drying dishes.

____ 5. The topic is
   A. uses of bandannas.
   B. uses of bandannas on camping trips.
   C. helpful things to take on a camping trip.

____ 6. The main idea is stated in sentence
   A. 1.   B. 2.   C. 4.

(Continues on next page)

¹There are various influences on how long we live. ²Some may surprise you. ³According to one researcher, if all cancer were suddenly cured, the average length of life would increase by less than two years. ⁴So why do we live twenty or thirty years longer than we used to? ⁵The answer, says this researcher, is that the number of childhood deaths has been greatly reduced. ⁶He says there is one thing we can do ourselves to lengthen our lives: exercise. ⁷Regular exercise would increase the average person's life by two or three years.

___ 7. The topic is
    A. cancer.
    B. how long we live.
    C. exercise.

___ 8. The main idea is stated in sentence
    A. 1.   B. 3.   C. 6.

¹What do Americans expect their schools to achieve? ²One commonly agreed-upon goal of education is the creation of good and effective citizens. ³A second goal is the possibility for economic advancement for students. ⁴For a long time, Americans have associated education with good jobs. ⁵Most students in colleges and universities are there to prepare for better careers. ⁶The third goal people count on their schools to accomplish is students' personal development—intellectual, emotional, and social. ⁷Thus there are three main goals Americans expect their schools to achieve.

___ 9. The topic is
    A. school goals.
    B. Americans.
    C. good citizens.

___10. The main idea is stated in sentence
    A. 1.   B. 2.   C. 7.

SUPPORTING DETAILS: Test A

A. (1–6.) Each group of items below includes a main idea and two major supporting details. In the space provided, label each item with one of the following:

    MI—for the **main idea**
    SD—for a **supporting detail**

Group 1

_____ A. There are some things to remember when filling out a job application.

_____ B. Make sure your writing is neat enough to read easily.

_____ C. Come prepared to fill in commonly requested information.

Group 2

_____ A. Young Amish boys learn to help their fathers tend crops and livestock.

_____ B. Amish children are taught to assist their parents with family work.

_____ C. Amish girls are taught to help their mothers cook, clean, and sew.

B. (7–10.) In the spaces provided, complete the outline of the paragraph by filling in the two missing major details. Then answer the questions that follow the outline. To help you focus on the details, the sentence expressing the main idea has been boldfaced.

    [1]**The First Community Bank is pleased to offer several types of checking accounts.** [2]First is our Regular Checking service, which requires a minimum balance of $250 in order to avoid monthly fees of $5.00 plus 25 cents per check issued. [3]No interest is earned on Regular Checking accounts. [4]Next is the Special Checking service. [5]If a minimum balance of $500 is maintained throughout the month, this type of account earns 4.5 percent. [6]Should the balance drop below $500, the fees listed for the Regular Checking accounts will apply until the balance once again reaches $500. [7]Finally, there's our Money Market Checking service. [8]A minimum balance of $2500 is required. [9]Money in this account earns 6.5 percent. [10]Three checks may be written on this Money Market account each month.

Main idea: Three types of checking accounts are offered by the First Community Bank.

    1. Regular Checking

    2. _____

    3. _____

9. Which addition word introduces the second major detail? _____

10. Which addition word introduces the last major detail?   _____

SUPPORTING DETAILS: Test B

A. (1–5.) Complete the outline of the paragraph below by adding the missing words to the main idea and filling in the missing major details. Then answer the questions that follow the outline. To help you focus on the supporting details, the sentence expressing the main idea has been boldfaced.

¹According to the saying "Spare the rod and spoil the child," harsh punishment is good for a child. ²**However, research shows that harsh punishment of a child can have undesired effects.** ³First of all, if a child is punished harshly by parents and teachers, a dislike for them is likely to develop. ⁴The child will tend to avoid activities associated with the parents and teachers. ⁵Family activities and school studies could thus become unpopular. ⁶Second, since punishment is generally either painful or frustrating, it can lead to aggression. ⁷One study showed boys who were severely punished for aggression at home tended to be overly aggressive in school. ⁸A third problem with harsh punishment is that repeated physical punishments can result in child abuse.

Main idea: Harsh punishment of a child _____

_____ .

   1. A dislike of parents and teachers and activities associated with them

   2. _____

   3. _____

____ 4. Which addition word or words introduce the first major detail?
   A. *For*
   B. *One*
   C. *First of all*

5. Which addition word introduces the last major detail? _____

(Continues on next page)

B. (6–10.) Complete the map of the following paragraph. First, add the missing words to the main idea at the top. Then complete and fill in the major details. Finally, answer the question that follows the map.

(To help you focus on the supporting details, find and underline the sentence expressing the main idea. You will also find it helpful to number or check the major details.)

¹Few products last forever. ²Most products go through a product life cycle, passing through four distinct stages in sales and earnings. ³The first stage in the product life cycle is the introductory stage. ⁴During this first stage, the producer tries to stir up demand. ⁵Typically, this phase involves expensive advertising and promotion, plus research and development costs. ⁶Next comes the growth stage, marked by a rapid jump in sales as the introductory efforts start paying off. ⁷As the product enters the growth phase, competition increases and the war for market share begins. ⁸This increased competition creates pressure to maintain large promotional budgets and reduce prices. ⁹During the third stage, the maturity stage, product sales begin to level off or show a slight decline. ¹⁰The key to success in the maturity phase is to encourage sales of the existing product by broadening its appeal or making minor improvements. ¹¹Although maturity can be extended for many years, sooner or later most products enter the decline stage. ¹²During this last phase, sales and profits begin to slip and eventually fade away.

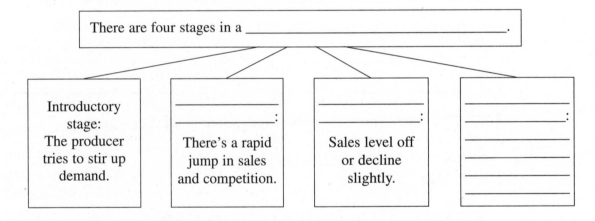

____10. The addition word that introduces the second major detail is

A. *second.*

B. *next.*

C. *plus.*

SUPPORTING DETAILS: Test C

Read each paragraph below, and then answer the questions that follow. To help you focus on the supporting details, the sentences expressing the main ideas have been boldfaced.

A. [1]Babe Ruth was known as the "Sultan of Swat" for his ability to hit lots of home runs. **[2]But he probably wouldn't have hit nearly as many if the major leagues hadn't made three key changes in 1920.** [3]One change was that pitchers were no longer allowed to throw spitballs. [4]Applying spit to a baseball makes it move in such a way that it becomes harder to hit. [5]Another key change was that a baseball that was even lightly scuffed was removed from play. [6]This change forced pitchers to work with tight, shiny new baseballs that were harder to grip. [7]A final change was in how baseballs were made: a better brand of yarn had become available that could be wound more tightly. [8]A baseball made of tightly wound yarn would travel farther when hit.

____ 1. As the main idea sentence suggests, the supporting details of this paragraph are
   A. reasons Babe Ruth was a great baseball player.
   B. changes that enabled baseball players to hit more home runs.
   C. reasons why baseball increased in popularity in 1920.

____ 2. According to the paragraph, scuffed baseballs
   A. travel farther when hit.
   B. are easier to grip.
   C. are easier to hit.

B. [1]One purpose of a census is to count the number of people living in a household. [2]A household is defined as all the persons living in a single house or apartment. **[3]Censuses around the world reveal a significant contrast between the average household sizes in various countries.** [4]In the United States, the average household has 3.1 persons. [5]That's a small average, but not the smallest in the world. [6]Sweden has the smallest, with an average of just 2.6 persons. [7]The country with the largest household of any North or South American country is Colombia, with 5.9 persons. [8]The country with the largest average household in the world is Gambia, in Africa. [9]There, the average household contains 8.3 persons.

____ 3. The major details of this paragraph are
   A. the average household size in various countries.
   B. purposes of a census.
   C. countries in North and South America.

____ 4. The country with the smallest average household in the world is
   A. the United States.
   B. Colombia.
   C. Sweden.

(Continues on next page)

_____ 5. The country with the largest average household in the world is
    A. Colombia.
    B. the United States.
    C. Gambia.

C. ¹**According to one author, nonverbal communication has four functions.** ²First of all, nonverbal cues may add to the meaning of a verbal message. ³When you meet someone for the first time, you might say, "I am really glad to meet you. ⁴I've heard a lot about you." ⁵If you say this with a warm smile and shake the person's hand, your nonverbal behavior adds to the words you have said. ⁶Second, nonverbal cues can regulate verbal communication. ⁷If you are talking to your boss or one of your teachers, how does she tell you that it's time for the conversation to end? ⁸She might get up out of her chair, or she might look pointedly at the clock on the wall—two ways to indicate that the conversation is over. ⁹A third function of nonverbal messages is to substitute for verbal messages. ¹⁰The secretary waves you into the boss's office without speaking. ¹¹We raise a hand in greeting instead of saying hello, or we give someone a hug—a wordless way of saying we like that person. ¹²Finally, nonverbal messages accent what we are saying. ¹³The politican pounds the lectern to make sure everyone realizes his or her message is important. ¹⁴A mother tells a child he is a bad boy and shakes a finger at him to emphasize the point. ¹⁵Whenever people are communicating something they consider important, they are likely to accent it with a nonverbal message.

_____ 6. An example of nonverbal communication is
    A. saying, "I am really glad to meet you. I've heard a lot about you."
    B. talking to your boss.
    C. giving someone a hug.

_____ 7. A nonverbal message is likely to be used for accent by a person
    A. who is too busy to speak.
    B. who says something he or she considers important.
    C. who wishes to end a conversation.

8. Fill in the blank: The addition word that introduces the last major detail of the paragraph is _____.

9–10. Complete the following outline of the paragraph by filling in the missing major details.

Main idea: Nonverbal communication has four functions.

1. To add to the meaning of a verbal message

2. To regulate verbal communication

3. _____

4. _____

SUPPORTING DETAILS: Test D

Outline the supporting points in each of the following paragraphs. Then answer the questions that follow the outline.

A. [1]Researchers in the field of communications have identified four kinds of listening. [2]One is listening for pleasure or enjoyment, as when we listen to music, to a comedy routine, or to an entertaining speech. [3]A second form of listening is to provide emotional support for the speaker, as when a psychiatrist listens to a patient or when we lend a sympathetic ear to a friend who is upset about something. [4]Another form of listening is to understand the message of a speaker, as when we attend a classroom lecture or listen to directions for finding a friend's house. [5]Finally, we listen for the purpose of accepting or rejecting a message, as when we listen to the sales pitch of a used-car dealer, the campaign speech of a political candidate, or the closing arguments of an attorney in a jury trial.

Main idea: There are four kinds of listening.

1. _____

2. _____

3. _____

4. _____

5. The addition words that signal the four major supporting details are as follows:

_____   _____   _____   _____

(Continues on next page)

B. (6–8.) Outline the supporting points in the following paragraph.

¹When people are hypnotized, they become very relaxed and open to suggestions. ²There are several common uses for hypnosis. ³To begin with, some hypnotists put people under a trance to entertain others. ⁴Hypnotists call volunteers from the audience and hypnotize them to act in funny ways. ⁵For example, they may make a person bark like a dog or do a funny dance. ⁶A second use for hypnosis is to help people to remember something important. ⁷If a crime was committed, a forgetful victim may be hypnotized to remember important details. ⁸The details help the police solve the crime. ⁹Sometimes hypnosis helps people in therapy remember painful things that they have forgotten from their childhood. ¹⁰Once that hidden pain comes out, a person can work on healing. ¹¹A last use for hypnosis is to help people overcome addictions or fears. ¹²A hypnotized person may be given powerful suggestions that help the person deal with the things he or she is addicted to or afraid of.

Main idea: There are several common uses for hypnosis.

1. _____

2. _____

3. _____

9. Which addition word or words introduce the first major detail?

   _____

10. Which addition word or words introduce the third major detail?

   _____

Name: _____

Section_____ Date_____

SCORE: (Number correct) × 20 = _____%

FINDING MAIN IDEAS: Test A

The main idea may appear at any place within each of the five paragraphs that follow. Write the number of each main idea sentence in the space provided.

1. [1]Adults can teach children to handle money in several ways. [2]For instance, children can be shown how to save money for special events such as birthdays or anniversaries. [3]They can also be taught how to open a bank account where their money can collect interest. [4]In addition, parents can help children agree on a guideline for using a little of the money for minor purchases such as candy or toys.

    Main idea sentence: _____

2. [1]Many people love to play and watch golf. [2]Yet golf is a very strange game. [3]In this game, you hit a ball and then go after it. [4]Even if you hit a terrible shot, you are forced to find your ball and continue using it. [5]Your goal is to hit the ball into a very small hole. [6]However, once you do this, you must remove the ball and go through the same routine seventeen more times.

    Main idea sentence: _____

3. [1]Long ago, many people couldn't read. [2]As a result, the news was often spread by word of mouth rather than through printed materials. [3]Town criers called out the day's news: births and weddings, deaths and bankruptcies, lists of lost property, and the like. [4]Official news was spread by men on horseback, dressed in the colors of the town or city. [5]Traveling merchants often passed along news concerning the rise and fall of prices, and the availability of certain goods.

    Main idea sentence: _____

4. [1]Americans are definitely eating more healthful meals. [2]We consume greater amounts than we used to of high-fiber foods, such as fruits and vegetables. [3]High-fiber foods are believed to help prevent certain cancers and other diseases. [4]Also, we are substituting low-fat foods for the higher-fat foods we used to eat. [5]For example, we may drink skim milk instead of whole milk. [6]Fatty foods contribute to a variety of serious ailments. [7]However, between meals, we often go back to eating large amounts of high-fat, low-fiber foods. [8]For instance, sales of ice cream and potato chips are enormous. [9]Apparently, we try hard to eat healthfully at mealtimes, but then undo some of the good work by "rewarding" ourselves with snacks that are bad for us.

    Main idea sentence: _____

(Continues on next page)

5. ¹Efforts to limit the use of tobacco began long before the present. ²For example, in 1646, Massachusetts passed a law limiting smoking because of the dangers of fire in the wooden homes of the time. ³A person could then legally smoke in Massachusetts only when traveling and no closer to a town than five miles. ⁴In 1647, Connecticut also passed a law limiting smoking, apparently for moral reasons. ⁵It banned social smoking. ⁶It also limited the use of tobacco to once a day and then only if the smoker was alone in his own home.

Main idea sentence: _____

FINDING MAIN IDEAS: Test B

The main idea may appear at any place within each of the five paragraphs that follow. Write the number of each main idea sentence in the space provided.

1. ¹Although there have been many great baseball players, none can top Hall of Fame pitcher Rube Waddell for strange and colorful behavior. ²For instance, Waddell had the bad habit of leaving the stadium in the middle of games to follow passing fire trucks to fires. ³Waddell was also known to enjoy playing marbles under the stands at game time while his teammates searched for their starting pitcher. ⁴Waddell was so bad at holding onto money that the Philadelphia Athletics once paid him his yearly salary in dollar bills, in the hope that he would spend it more slowly.

    Main idea sentence: _____

2. ¹These days we are encouraged to recycle at least some of our solid waste by disposing of it in specially marked containers. ²In early American cities, however, people used hogs to recycle solid waste. ³The hogs consumed the mixture of garbage, manure, and human slop that filled open gutters and converted it into flesh to be consumed by the people who owned them. ⁴In New York City, for example, apartment dwellers relied on these animals as a main source of meat, and butchers "ran" pigs through the streets to fatten them for free.

    Main idea sentence: _____

3. ¹Severe winter storms can be dramatic, beautiful—and dangerous. ²A few simple precautions, however, can reduce the discomfort and damage a storm can cause. ³A severe blizzard can disrupt electrical service, leaving homes without light or heat. ⁴When electric heat is shut down, wood stoves or fireplaces can help, but charcoal should never be used as an indoor fuel because burning it produces a poisonous gas. ⁵If the heat will be off for some time, it's a good idea to drain water pipes to prevent them from freezing. ⁶Water expands when it freezes, so frozen pipes can burst. ⁷Also, heavy snow can block streets, confining people to their homes for several days at a time. ⁸A supply of canned goods—and a manual can opener—can be a valuable asset to a snowbound family.

    Main idea sentence: _____

(Continues on next page)

4. ¹With a device called a teletypewriter, or TTY, deaf people can communicate on the telephone using the written word rather than the voice. ²Two people with this equipment converse by dialing the phone number in the usual way. ³Then they type out their message on the keyboard of the TTY. ⁴The message is transmitted over the telephone line and gets printed out on a screen or paper, depending on the type of TTY used. ⁵The receiver can then type back a message to the original caller, and so on.

    Main idea sentence: _____

5. ¹If a naked woman rode down your street on a horse, could you resist taking a look? ²That's the decision a tailor in Coventry, England, had to make in the eleventh century. ³The governor of his town was making the people pay too much in taxes. ⁴The governor's wife, Godiva, asked him to have mercy on the people. ⁵He agreed, if she would ride through the streets naked, and that's what Lady Godiva did. ⁶All the people in town covered their windows so that they would not embarrass the lady. ⁷But one tailor, Tom, took a look. ⁸And so ever since Lady Godiva's naked ride, the term "Peeping Tom" has meant someone who spies on other people.

    Main idea sentence: _____

Name: _____

Section_____ Date _____

SCORE: (Number correct) × 20 = _____%

FINDING MAIN IDEAS: Test C

The main idea may appear at any place within each of the five paragraphs that follow. Write the number of each main idea sentence in the space provided.

1. ¹Like many other features of communication, eye contact is influenced by cultural background. ²When engaged in conversation, Arabs, Latin Americans, and Southern Europeans tend to look directly at the person with whom they are talking. ³People from Asian countries and parts of Africa tend to engage in less eye contact. ⁴In Kenya, a discussion between a woman and her son-in-law may well be conducted with each person turning his or her back to the other!

   Main idea sentence: _____

2. ¹It's hard to imagine bees and wasps that can't fly. ²But, say researchers, bees, wasps, and other insects developed the ability to fly gradually. ³Millions of years ago, insects had small "wings" that they used as solar panels. ⁴These panels let the insects capture more warmth from the sun. ⁵In cooler weather, insects moved their wings faster in order to gain more warmth. ⁶Insects with large wings thus survived better in all temperatures, causing the wings to get larger and larger through the generations. ⁷Eventually, the wings were large enough to allow the insects to fly.

   Main idea sentence: _____

3. ¹In the seventeenth century, the Dutch became very fond of collecting tulip bulbs. ²The finest bulbs gained high prices, and traders began making a profit in buying and selling them. ³Eventually, people paid great fortunes for single tulip bulbs, kept them for a few weeks, and then sold them for even a higher price. ⁴But finally, buyers realized that the bulbs were not worth the high prices demanded. ⁵The great Tulip Mania came to a sudden end when prices fell greatly overnight. ⁶The common Dutch tulip thus led to one of the first "crashes" in economic history.

   Main idea sentence: _____

4. ¹People who are convicted of robbing or burglarizing strangers are likely to be sent to prison. ²But police officers and prosecutors tend to regard crimes between acquaintances less seriously than other crimes. ³For example, suppose that Joe and Dan know each other. ⁴Dan steals Joe's TV set, and claims he did it because Joe didn't pay back money that Dan had lent him. ⁵This is likely to be regarded as a sort of private matter—Joe may not be considered altogether innocent by the police and prosecutor. ⁶And Dan is less likely to be sent to prison than if he had stolen the TV from someone he didn't know.

   Main idea sentence: _____   *(Continues on next page)*

5. ¹Many people say that mystery stories are their favorite form of reading. ²Perhaps that's because almost all mystery stories follow a certain formula. ³For one thing, all mystery stories feature a detective. ⁴One famous early detective was Sherlock Holmes, and he has been followed by thousands more. ⁵Secondly, all mystery stories feature a crime. ⁶This crime is sometimes, but not always, murder. ⁷Many mysteries have involved robberies of some sort. ⁸Some recent ones even feature environmental crimes. ⁹Thirdly, all mystery stories feature clues and evidence that enable the reader to reason along with the detective to solve the crime. ¹⁰In addition, most mysteries feature a limited number of suspects, so people have a better chance to guess at just who the villain might be. ¹¹Finally, mysteries offer the reader a solution. ¹²That's when we learn, once and for all, "whodunit."

Main idea sentence: _____

Name: _____

Section_____ Date _____

SCORE: (Number correct) × 20 = _____%

FINDING MAIN IDEAS: Test D

The main idea may appear at any place within each of the five paragraphs that follow. Write the number of each main idea sentence in the space provided.

1. [1]Nearly everyone considers Abraham Lincoln to be one of our greatest presidents. [2]But Lincoln might never have become president if he had actually fought the duel he had been challenged to as a young man. [3]It happened like this: On September 2, 1842, Lincoln wrote a letter to an Illinois newspaper which criticized the political views and the personal vanity of a political opponent named James Shields. [4]Shields, who was rather vain, especially when it came to the ladies, was furious and challenged Lincoln to a duel. [5]Lincoln accepted. [6]Fortunately for both men, several of their friends begged them to let the matter drop. [7]Their pleas worked, and the duel was cancelled at the last moment. [8]And as we all know, Lincoln went on to greatness.

   Main idea sentence: _____

2. [1]Children who are neglected or abused in early childhood can be damaged to a degree that can never be fully repaired. [2]One little girl known as Anna is a sad example. [3]Anna was the illegitimate child of a young woman living in a rural area in the 1940s. [4]The child's mother confined her to a dark attic room, where she was given enough milk to live, but almost no human contact. [5]When Anna was 6, she was discovered by the authorities and placed in a foster home. [6]At that time, she appeared to be deaf and profoundly mentally retarded, being unable to walk, talk, or even chew. [7]Eventually Anna began to learn to walk and talk, but she never achieved anything approaching normal development. [8]Her early malnutrition led to her death at age 11.

   Main idea sentence: _____

3. [1]When you think of surveys, you may recall seeing many "person on the street" interviews on local television news shows. [2]While such interviews can be highly entertaining, they are not necessarily an accurate indication of public opinion. [3]First, they reflect the opinions of only those people who happen to be at a certain location. [4]Such a sample can be biased in favor of commuters, middle-class shoppers, or factory workers, depending on which street or area the newspeople select. [5]Second, television interviews tend to attract outgoing people who are willing to appear on the air, while they frighten away others who may feel intimidated by a camera.

   Main idea sentence: _____

(Continues on next page)

4. ¹In naturally stressful situations, the time of greatest stress is not necessarily the time when danger is at its height. ²Seymour Epsin illustrated this when he studied the pattern of stress on a group of twenty-eight parachutists. ³Each man was asked to describe his feelings before, during, and after his jump. ⁴All reported an increase of fear and of desire to escape as the time for the jump approached. ⁵Once the men were in line and realized that they could not turn back, however, they began to calm down. ⁶By the time they reached the most dangerous part of the jump—when they were in freefall and waiting for their chutes to open—they had calmed down.

Main idea sentence: _____

5. ¹A researcher traveled all over the world filming the flirting behavior of many different cultures. ²He found that flirters everywhere move closer than normal to the person they're flirting with. ³They also allow their hands to lightly brush against the other person. ⁴Another common flirting behavior, he noted, is frequently moistening one's lips. ⁵In addition, flirting people keep their mouths slightly open, and look into the other's eyes just slightly longer than is usual. ⁶Also, flirters in all cultures direct slight smiles and bashful looks towards the one they're attracted to. ⁷Finally, he found that flirting people everywhere try to find subjects of conversation about which they and the other person will agree. ⁸Clearly, flirting is done much the same in different cultures.

Main idea sentence: _____

Name: _____

Section_____ Date_____

SCORE: (Number correct) × 10 = _____%

SIGNAL WORDS I: Test A

A. Fill in each blank with an appropriate signal word from the box. Use each transition once. Then, in the space provided, write the letter of the signal word you have chosen.

A. also	B. as	C. during
D. in addition	E. then	

___ 1. Oprah Winfrey's idea of a perfect world includes great respect for children. She

_____ feels that in a perfect world, schools would teach people to

take responsibility for their own actions.

___ 2. Lungs take oxygen from the air and _____ pump it into your blood system.

___ 3. _____ the Middle Ages, people believed that the heart, not the brain,

was the center of intelligence.

___ 4. Crying provides an emotional release. _____, it is a release of the

tensions that led up to your feeling like crying.

___ 5. "Long in the tooth," meaning "old," was originally used to describe horses.

_____ horses age, their gums recede, giving the impression that their

teeth are growing. The longer the teeth look, the older the horse.

B. (6–9.) Fill in each blank with an appropriate signal word from the box. Use each transition once.

afterward	during	when
while		

[1]A father Emperor penguin withstands the Antarctic cold for 60 days or more

to protect his eggs, which he keeps on his feet, covered with a feathered flap.

[2](6)_____ this entire time, he doesn't eat a thing. [3]Most father

penguins lose about 25 pounds (7)_____ they wait for their

babies to hatch. [4](8)_____, they feed the chicks a special liquid

from their throats. [5](9)_____ the mother penguins return to care

for the young, the fathers go to sea to eat and rest. [6]Clearly, male Emperor penguins

are devoted fathers, at least while their offspring are very young.

___10. This paragraph uses
    A. addition words.   B. time words.

SIGNAL WORDS I: Test B

A. Fill in each blank with an appropriate signal word from the box. Use each transition once. Then, in the space provided, write the letter of the signal word you have chosen.

A. another	B. during	C. first of all
D. in addition	E. one	

____ 1. Common symptoms of food poisoning are nausea and diarrhea. _____, a person might have a headache, fever, or chills.

____ 2. At one time, people thought that disease was caused by demons. At _____, they saw it as a form of punishment for moral weakness.

____ 3. _____ the dry season, an elephant will dig holes to find underground springs.

____ 4. Casual sex is risky for a number of reasons. _____, it increases the chances of getting a sexually transmitted disease.

____ 5. There are several ways to reduce eyestrain due to heavy computer use. _____ is to try blinking your eyes lightly and often.

B. (6–10.) Fill in each blank with an appropriate transition from the box. Use each transition once.

another	later	moreover
one	then	

[1]New arenas are being built to be useful for many kinds of functions. [2](6)_____ use is as a multi-sport arena. [3]For instance, a hockey game may be played in the afternoon. [4](7)_____ a basketball game can be played in the same place (8)_____ in the evening. [5](9)_____ use of the new arenas is for concerts. [6](10)_____, small conventions can also be held in these new arenas.

SIGNAL WORDS I: Test C

A. (1–3.) Fill in each blank with an appropriate addition word from the box. Use each transition once.

another	one	third

¹Salt contains sodium, which can be dangerous to one's health. ²For this reason, scientists have suggested ways for people to cut back on the use of salt in their diet. ³(1)_____ way to do this is to eat more natural foods—that is, fruits and vegetables. ⁴(2)_____ is to read labels and buy products that are low in salt or contain no salt. ⁵A (3)_____ way to cut down on salt is to use plenty of spices so that less salt is needed for flavor.

B. (4–6.) Fill in each blank with an appropriate time word from the box. Use each transition once.

finally	next	then

¹On a hot, humid day, a person's body may be overworked, and sunstroke may occur. ²To treat sunstroke, move the victim into a cool place such as an air-conditioned room. ³(4)_____, remove the person's clothing and wrap him or her in a cool, wet sheet. ⁴(5)_____ fan the person until the body temperature falls below 101 degrees. ⁵(6)_____, replace the wet sheet with a dry one.

⁶If the person's temperature rises above 101 degrees again, repeat the procedure.

(Continues on next page)

C. (7–9.) Fill in each blank with an appropriate word from the box. Use each transition once.

after	later	when

¹The presidential election of 2000 was decided by a single state: Florida. ²At first, television election coverage declared that Al Gore had won the state. ³But by the early hours of the morning, it was clear that this election was still in doubt. ⁴(7)_____ the Florida votes were first tallied, George Bush narrowly edged out Gore, but by so close a margin that an automatic recount was legally required. ⁵Charges and countercharges flew. ⁶(8)_____ thirty-six days of confusion, the Supreme Court voted 5 to 4 to end the recount process. ⁷Florida's electoral votes—and the presidency—went to George Bush. ⁸A little over two years (9)_____, under his direction, the United States began the Iraq War.

___10. This paragraph uses
    A. addition words.   B. time words.

SIGNAL WORDS I: Test D

A. Fill in each blank with an appropriate time word from the box. Use each transition once.

during	later	while

[1]In 1921, the Declaration of Independence and the Constitution of the United States were displayed in the Library of Congress. [2]However, (1)_____ World War II, the documents were brought for safekeeping to Fort Knox. [3](2)_____ at Fort Knox, the Declaration was repaired by experts, who filled in microscopic holes and cracks in the parchment. [4]Near the end of the war, the documents were brought back to the Library of Congress. [5]About eight years (3)_____, they were moved to the newly built National Archives building.

____ 4. This paragraph uses
    A. addition words.   B. time words.

B. Read the paragraph below and answer the questions that follow.

[1]Leaders are people who influence the behavior of others. [2]But what is the source of their power? [3]Researchers have found five types of power that give leaders influence. [4]First is the power to reward. [5]In work organizations, rewards can come in the form of promotions or pay raises. [6]Another source of influence is the ability to punish. [7]In a work organization, a leader can punish people by refusing to give them a raise or even by firing them. [8]A third source of a leader's influence is organizational power. [9]Organizational power exists in highly structured organizations, such as the military. [10]In the military, for instance, the lower ranks must always obey the higher ranks. [11]Expert power is the fourth source of influence. [12]Expert power is gained with knowledge. [13]For instance, the leader of a study group will probably be the person who knows more about the topic being studied than others. [14]The final source of leadership influence is personality power. Leaders with this type of power are looked up to and admired by others.

____ 5. This paragraph uses
    A. addition words.   B. time words.

6–10. Complete the outline of the selection by filling in the key supporting details.

    Main idea: Five types of power give leaders influence.

    1. _____

    2. _____

    3. _____

    4. _____

    5. _____

SIGNAL WORDS II: Test A

A. Fill in each blank with an appropriate signal word from the box. Use each transition once. Then, in the space provided, write the letter of the signal word you have chosen.

A. however	B. on the other hand	C. result
D. since	E. such as	

___ 1. The artist Vincent Van Gogh sold only one painting in his lifetime. Today, _____, his paintings sell for millions of dollars.

___ 2. My best friends share important characteristics, _____ honesty and a sense of humor.

___ 3. It was once believed that pregnant women could increase their chances of bearing sons if they ate red meat and salty snacks. _____, eating vegetables and sweet snacks was supposed to increase the odds of having daughters.

___ 4. _____ my neighbor and I both work for the same company, we have decided to car pool.

___ 5. Many American men believe that they are not supposed to show emotions. As a _____, according to research, only one male in ten has a close male friend with whom he shares his innermost thoughts.

B. (6–8.) Fill in each blank with an appropriate signal word from the box. Use each transition once.

causes	leads to	reason

[1]When you awaken in the morning, you are about one-half inch taller than when you went to bed. [2]The (6)_____ for this change stems from the fact that you have fluid-filled discs in your spine. [3]When you are upright—either sitting or standing—gravity squeezes down the fluid, which (7)_____ your back to become shorter. [4]During the night, when you are lying down, the discs gradually spring back to their regular "unsquashed" size, which (8)_____ greater height.

(Continues on next page)

C. (9–10.) Fill in each blank with an appropriate signal word from the box. Use each transition once.

instance	for example

[1]The foot-in-the door technique involves getting people to agree to a small request to increase the chances that they will agree to a larger request later. [2](9)_____, groups seeking donations often ask people to simply sign a petition first. [3]Salespeople commonly ask individuals to try a product with "no obligation" before they launch their hard sell. [4]Another (10)_____ of the foot-in-the-door technique would be when a wife asks her husband to get her a cup of coffee, then when he gets up to fetch it, saying, "While you're up, would you fix me a peanut butter sandwich?"

Name: _____

Section_____ Date_____

SCORE: (Number correct) × 10 = _____%

SIGNAL WORDS II: Test B

A. Fill in each blank with an appropriate signal word from the box. Use each transition once. Then, in the space provided, write the letter of the signal word you have chosen.

A. as a result	B. because	C. despite
D. for example	E. including	

____ 1. People came to American for many reasons. _____, my grandparents came because they had heard that the streets in America were paved with gold.

____ 2. _____ interviewers generally pay more attention to negative information than to positive information, applicants should be careful not to volunteer negative information.

____ 3. The kiwi, national bird of New Zealand, can't fly. It lives in a hole in the ground, is almost blind, and lays only one egg each year. _____ all this, it has survived for more than 70 million years.

____ 4. Certain extremely popular books, _____ the Bible, the Koran, and Dr. Spock's *Baby and Child Care,* have never gone out of print.

____ 5. _____ of health issues, cigarettes' share of vending machine sales have gone from 25% to just 2% in the past 25 years.

B. (6–7.) Fill in each blank with an appropriate signal word from the box. Use each transition once.

on the other hand	while

[1](6)_____ some diseases have struck humanity since its earliest history, other diseases are new. [2]For instance, some of the bones discovered in prehistoric caves show evidence of arthritis. [3]Cancer is also very old; it was described and named by the ancient Greeks about 2,500 years ago. [4](7)_____, AIDS is a new disease, discovered as recently as 1981. [5]Legionnaire's disease, which affects the lungs, is also new, having first appeared in 1976.

(Continues on next page)

C. (8–9.) Fill in each blank with an appropriate signal word from the box. Use each transition once.

different	in contrast

¹Although they are sometimes confused, envy and jealousy are two (8)_____ emotions. ²Envy is a desire to get something that another person possesses. ³Usually, this occurs in situations in which people we like or associate with have things or take actions that threaten our definition of ourselves. ⁴Someone who defines himself or herself as successful might become envious if a coworker was given a larger raise, a relative purchased a more expensive car, or a friend received a higher grade point average. ⁵(9)_____, jealousy is a fear of losing something to which we have become attached. ⁶We are jealous when we fear losing a dating partner or spouse to another person or when we feel excluded from the company of someone we like or love.

____10. This paragraph uses
   A. contrast words.
   B. cause and effect words.
   C. example words.

SIGNAL WORDS II: Test C

A. (1–3.) Fill in each blank with an appropriate signal word from the box. Use each transition once.

result	since	therefore

[1]Grocery shopping has changed greatly since the 1800s. [2]Nineteenth-century shopkeepers feared theft, so all products were located on one side of a counter, out of the reach of customers. [3]Customers had to ask for or point to what they wanted. [4]Also, many foods did not come in individually wrapped consumer-size packages. [5](1)_____, an assistant had to measure out the exact amount desired by the consumer. [6]The shopping process was slow (2)_____ the number of customers who could be helped at one time was limited by the number of clerks employed in the store. [7]When self-serve supermarkets became popular in the 1940s, grocers made up for money lost as the (3)_____ of shoplifting with lower labor costs and increased sales.

___ 4. This paragraph uses time words and

    A. example words.   B. cause and effect words.   C. contrast words.

B. (5–6.) Fill in each blank with an appropriate signal word from the box. Use each transition once.

different	while

[1]How much is a serving? [2]Is it (5)_____ from a portion? [3]While these two terms often are used interchangeably, they actually mean different things. [4]A serving is the amount of food recommended in materials such as the Food Guide Pyramid, (6)_____ a portion is the amount of food you choose to eat at any one time and that may be more or less than a serving. [5]Most people have trouble judging what a serving looks like and eat two to three servings when they think they are having only one. [6]In a national survey, more than half of Americans overestimated the serving size of cooked pasta and rice, and took at least twice the amount that they should have.

___ 7. This paragraph uses

    A. example words.   B. cause and effect words.   C. contrast words.

(Continues on next page)

C. (8–10.) Complete the outline of the following paragraph.

¹Why are Americans so stressed out? ²According to researchers, there are four basic reasons. ³One explanation is that more workers are employed in service industries. ⁴Workers in these jobs must deal with a variety of people on a daily basis. ⁵While most customers are easy to deal with, some are difficult. ⁶This leads to stress. ⁷Another factor which causes stress is that the economy is unpredictable. ⁸In the age of takeovers, downsizing, and bankruptcies, even excellent workers often fear losing their jobs. ⁹Third, rapid changes in computer technology force workers to develop new skills and do so quickly. ¹⁰Some changes in computer technology also lead to layoffs. ¹¹Finally, because the workplace is becoming more diverse, individuals from all groups must learn to interact with those who are unfamiliar. ¹²Developing these skills takes time and may be stressful.

Main idea: There are four factors which cause Americans to feel stressed.

1. _____

   _____

2. _____

   _____

3. _____

   _____

4. The workplace is becoming more diverse, requiring people to learn how to interact with others who are unfamiliar.

Name: _____

Section_____ Date_____

SCORE: (Number correct) × 10 = _____%

SIGNAL WORDS II: Test D

A. (1–4.) Fill in each blank with an appropriate signal word from the box. Use each transition once.

different	instead	on the other hand
rather than		

¹People have (1)_____ opinions as to whether zoos help or harm wild animals. ²Supporters of zoos argue that seeing zoo animals gives children an appreciation for wild animals that they might not otherwise have. ³They also believe that breeding programs in zoos help to ensure that no wild animal will ever become extinct. ⁴(2)_____, those who dislike zoos argue that it is cruel to enclose wild animals in zoos. ⁵They believe that zoo animals are prevented from living out their lives in a natural manner. ⁶They argue that, (3)_____ spending money on zoos, people should (4)_____ donate money to help ensure the safety of wild animals in their own natural environments.

B. (5–10.) Fill in each blank with an appropriate signal word from the box. Use each transition once.

affect	cause	due to
finally	led	secondly

¹According to one author, there appear to be three main factors which (5)_____ a president's popularity. ²The president's character clearly plays some part in the public's response. ³The belief that President Bill Clinton lacked moral standards (6)_____ his affair with a White House intern (7)_____ some Americans to disapprove of his presidency. ⁴(8)_____, economic factors affect how much support a president receives. ⁵A failed economy probably cost Presidents Gerald Ford, Jimmy Carter, and George H.W. Bush a second term, while Presidents Clinton and George W. Bush both benefited from a strengthened economy. ⁶(9)_____, international crises nearly always have the effect of increasing the president's public standing, at least temporarily. ⁷In the days after 9/11, President Bush's popularity soared to 85%. ⁸Yet ongoing crises can eventually (10)_____ a president to lose popular support. As the Iraq war entered its fifth year, President Bush's popularity dropped to under 30%.

Name: _____

Section_____ Date _____

SCORE: (Number correct) × 10 = _____%

INFERENCES: Test A

A. (1–2.) Put a check (✓) by the **two** inferences that are most logically based on the passage below.

> [1]One day a Native American chief told his grandchildren that there was a war going on inside him between two wolves: one, the wolf of kindness, and the other, the wolf of cruelty. [2]His grandchildren asked him which wolf would win the fight, and he said to them, "The wolf that will win is the wolf you feed."

____ A. While cruel treatment can make people cruel, kind treatment can make them kind.

____ B. The chief was hungry.

____ C. People must struggle not to give in to their worst natures.

____ D. The chief wanted to scare his grandchildren.

B. (3–8.) Put a check (✓) by the **two** inferences that are most logically based on each of the sentences below.

> • An army of sheep led by a lion would defeat an army of lions led by a sheep.
> —Arab proverb

____ A. Strong leadership is not all that important.

____ B. Some qualities are more important than physical strength.

____ C. Contrary to popular belief, sheep are as brave as lions.

____ D. People who are courageous can inspire even those who are fearful.

> • Our greatest glory is not in never falling, but in rising every time we fall.

____ E. It's better to succeed immediately than to succeed after long effort.

____ F. It's shameful to fail.

____ G. People have the most respect for those who overcome obstacles.

____ H. It's important to keep trying.

> • A hero is a man who does what he can. —Romain Rolland

____ I. Heroism doesn't always consist of noticeable actions.

____ J. Many people do not do all they can to help others.

____ K. It is easy to be a hero.

____ L. People have to be outstandingly brave to be heroic.

(Continues on next page)

C. (9–10.) Read the following passage and then check (✓) the **two** inferences that are most firmly based on the given information.

¹As a child, Rita Mae Brown wanted very much to be liked. ²That was a mistake she wrote about later: "The reward for conformity was that everyone liked you except yourself. ³Life is too short for conformity." ⁴In other words, Brown suggests that the only way to live a happy life is to be yourself. ⁵There will always be people in our lives—family, friends, co-workers, and so on—who make demands on our time and our behaviors. ⁶Although we can accept some of those requests, only we can know what will really work for us. ⁷This means that not everyone will like us. ⁸That is simply a fact of life that we all must come to accept. ⁹As Brown also points out, there is little time to waste when it comes to how we choose to live our lives. ¹⁰We are best served by following our own hearts and taking others' "advice" with, at the very least, a grain of salt. ¹¹Being unhappy is no reward; liking oneself is.

____ A. As a child, Rita Mae Brown tried hard to "fit in."

____ B. Rita Mae Brown believes that people should pay no attention to the demands of others.

____ C. Rita Mae Brown has few friends.

____ D. Rita Mae Brown has done things that displeased some people.

INFERENCES: Test B

A. (1–3.) Read the following passage and then check (✓) the **three** inferences that are most firmly based on the given information.

> [1]Author Mark Twain once spent three weeks fishing in the Maine woods, regardless of the fact that it was the state's closed season for fishing. [2]Relaxing in the lounge car of the train on his return journey to New York, his catch iced down in the baggage car, he looked for someone to whom he could relate the story of his successful holiday. [3]The stranger to whom he began to boast of his sizable catch appeared at first unresponsive, then positively grim.
>
> [4]"By the way, who are you, sir?" inquired Twain airily.
>
> [5]"I'm the state game warden," was the unwelcome response. [6]"Who are you?"
>
> [7]Twain nearly swallowed his cigar. [8]"Well, to be perfectly truthful, warden," he said hastily, "I'm the biggest damn liar in the whole United States."

____ A. Twain often broke the law.

____ B. Twain was embarrassed to have told the game warden that he had been fishing when he shouldn't have.

____ C. Twain loved to have an audience.

____ D. The game warden would not arrest Twain for fishing when he wasn't supposed to.

____ E. The game warden found Twain's story amusing.

____ F. After he learned the game warden's identity, Twain tried to convince him that he had been making up his story of a sizable catch.

B. (4–7.) Put a check (✓) by the **two** inferences that are most logically based on each of the sentences below.

- If you have built castles in the air, your work need not be lost; that is where they should be. Now put the foundations under them.

____ A. Dreaming is a waste of time.

____ B. It takes hard work to achieve one's dreams.

____ C. Dreaming about something is only the first step toward achieving it.

____ D. If you dream enough about something, it will happen.

- I don't know who my grandfather was; I am much more concerned to know what his grandson will be. —Abraham Lincoln

____ E. Abraham Lincoln is concerned not with who his grandfather was but who he himself will be.

____ F. The speaker was orphaned at an early age.

____ G. What we make of ourselves is more important than our family background.

____ H. The speaker hopes to one day meet his grandfather's grandson.

(Continues on next page)

C. (8–10.) Read the following passage and then check (✓) the **three** inferences that are most firmly based on the given information.

> [1]I was always hustling to make some money because my mother never gave me any. [2]I started delivering groceries when I was ten. [3]The grocer gave me a choice— ten cents an hour or three cents for every order I delivered. [4]I worked fast, so I took the three-cents-an-order deal. [5]But I soon realized that I'd made the wrong decision. [6]Every order he gave me was at least ten blocks from the store. [7]Two hours later, I told the guy, "No more three cents an order. [8]From now on, I'll take the ten-cents-an-hour deal." [9]He said okay.
>
> [10]Then he gave me six deliveries—all going to the same apartment house.
>
> [11]When I finished for the day and was ready to go home, the boss turned out to be a good guy. [12]He gave me an extra buck and a Swiss-cheese sandwich for the walk home. [13]The sandwich he made tasted real good. [14]He put something in it that I'd never had before—lettuce.
>
> —from Rodney Dangerfield, *It's Not Easy Bein' Me*

____ A. Dangerfield was lazy as a boy.

____ B. The author was very poor as a child.

____ C. Dangerfield's mother didn't want him to earn money because he was only ten.

____ D. It was a mistake for Dangerfield to change his mind about getting paid by the delivery.

____ E. Dangerfield realized that it's always better to get paid by the hour than by the delivery.

____ F. By the end of the day, the boss had changed his mind about how much to pay the author.

INFERENCES: Test C

A. (1–3.) Read the following passage and then check (✓) the **three** inferences that are most firmly based on the given information.

> [1]In July, 1885, the great French chemist Louis Pasteur created the first vaccine to treat rabies. [2]The event received only mild attention in American newspapers. [3]Then in early December, a rabid dog ran furiously through the streets of Newark, New Jersey, biting several other dogs and six young children. [4]At a time when hundreds of thousands of stray dogs lived in large cities, such events were commonplace. [5]But this was the first such disaster since Pasteur's announcement. [6]Within hours, a local doctor told the newspapers that the children's parents should take them to Paris immediately. [7]Since the parents of the boys were working-class, newspapers began a publicity campaign to raise the needed funds. [8]Within 24 hours, ordinary people had donated enough money to send the boys on a voyage to France. [9]When the boys returned healthy from Paris a few weeks later, they became the toast of the town—and the country. [10]Crowds paid ten cents just to hear the boys tell of their Atlantic voyages and how Pasteur had saved their lives.

____ A. Then, as now, the media can play an important part in getting the public to take action.

____ B. Poor people in the 1800s didn't often travel overseas.

____ C. The rabies vaccine has to be given to people within a few hours after they have been bitten by a rabid animal.

____ D. Life-threatening situations can sometimes bring out the best in people.

____ E. Louis Pasteur was the greatest scientist of the 19th century.

____ F. Many people did not believe the news that Pasteur had discovered a rabies vaccine.

B. (4–7.) Put a check (✓) by the **two** inferences that are most logically based on each of the sentences below.

> • God will not look you over for medals, degrees or diplomas, but for scars.

____ A. God wants people to take it easy.

____ B. A person's true worth is measured by how much he or she has overcome.

____ C. God is not greatly impressed by the rewards that people give to one another.

____ D. Courage and intelligence are unimportant qualities.

> • "It is better to know the patient who has the disease than it is to know the disease which the patient has." —Hippocrates

____ E. Above all, a doctor must understand diseases.

____ F. Doctors must be aware of a patient's thoughts and feelings.

____ G. Most diseases can be easily cured.

____ H. Doctors should treat all patients as individuals.

(Continues on next page)

C. (8–10.) Read the following passage and then check (✓) the **three** inferences that are most firmly based on the given information.

¹Let's say Mary comes home from work, upset and frustrated because her boss let her know that the project she had just completed did not adequately meet company standards. ²"There's just no pleasing that man! ³Whatever I do, it's just never good enough for him," she complains to her husband Tom. ⁴Tom responds by offering to go over the company guidelines with Mary and is confused when Mary bursts into tears and runs out of the room. ⁵"You just don't understand!" she shouts at him as she slams the bedroom door. ⁶Later Mary calls her friend Lena and tells her about the situation. ⁷Lena responds, "Oh I know just how you feel! ⁸I've had the same experience with my boss sometimes. ⁹After all the hard work you put into that project, it's so frustrating to be told it just doesn't hit the mark!" ¹⁰Mary sighs in relief and later spends the evening going over the project manual.

____ A. Mary was upset with Tom because he did not acknowledge her feelings.

____ B. Mary is not a good employee.

____ C. Tom does not want Mary to work outside the home.

____ D. Mary was pleased with Lena because Lena acknowledged her feelings.

____ E. Lena is more intelligent than Mary.

____ F. Mary takes her job very seriously.

INFERENCES: Test D

In the space provided, write the letter of the sentence that best expresses the implied main idea of each paragraph.

____ 1. [1]In 1992, Ray Krong was accused of murdering a waitress. [2]He was sentenced to death and spent ten years in prison. [3]Then, police did a DNA analysis. [4]They found out that another man was guilty of the crime. [5]Ray was released from prison because the DNA proved that he was innocent. [6]In 1979, a gas station worker named George was murdered. [7]A man named Joseph, who was in the service station, blamed the murder on someone else. [8]The crime was a mystery until twenty-two years later when the police did a DNA test. [9]The DNA test proved that George's blood was on Joseph's clothes. [10]Because of the DNA evidence, Joseph was found guilty and was sent to jail.

    A. Before DNA testing, police had no way of knowing who did or did not commit crimes.

    B. Thanks to DNA testing, innocent people no longer go to prison.

    C. DNA testing has become a valuable tool in law enforcement.

    D. DNA testing is most often used in cases involving murder.

____ 2. [1]During World War II, over 400,000 American women volunteered to serve in the armed forces. [2]They became nurses, pilots, and other service personnel. [3]Women who stayed at home also did their part. [4]Many women got jobs for the first time. [5]They kept the country running by taking over the jobs that men left behind. [6]Instead of being housewives, women became farmers, airplane mechanics, store managers, and other workers. [7]Some women volunteered to help out in service organizations. [8]They took donations and raised money to send supplies to the soldiers overseas. [9]Women conserved food and gas so that there would be enough for the war. [10]They also saved their nylon stockings and old lipstick tubes because the materials could be recycled and turned into weapons and supplies.

    A. During World War II, many American women worked outside the home for the first time.

    B. During World War II, many American women enlisted in the armed forces.

    C. During World War II, many American women were employed both in the armed forces and in private industry.

    D. During World War II, American women made a major contribution to the war effort.

____ 3. [1]Before electric power became widely available, houses were lit by kerosene lamps, whose wicks had to be trimmed just right or the lamp smoked or went out. [2]There were no bathrooms, because bathrooms required running water, and running water depended on an electric pump. [3]Women and children hauled water constantly—for infrequent baths, for continuous canning (because without a refrigerator, fruits and vegetables had to be preserved almost immediately, or they spoiled), and for wash day.

(Continues on next page)

[4]Wash day, always Monday, meant scrubbing clothes by hand with harsh soap on a washboard; it meant boiling clothes in a large copper vat over a woodstove and stirring them with a wooden fork. [5]It was a hot, backbreaking job, especially in summer.

   A. Before the invention of electric power, women and children hauled water constantly.

   B. Before the invention of electric power, doing chores at home was very difficult.

   C. Washing clothes was one of many backbreaking jobs that women did.

   D. Bathrooms became common with the invention of electric power.

___ 4. [1]Most people are familiar with dogs that help blind people by guiding them as they walk. [2]Similar to guide dogs, "hearing" or "signal" dogs are trained to help deaf people. [3]They alert their owners to sounds, usually by approaching the owner and then by going back to the source of the sound. [4]They signal such noises as doorbells, phones, smoke alarms, crying babies, microwave bells, and even tea kettles whistling. [5]Another kind of helping dog, "mobility assist" dogs, can pull a person's wheelchair, carry things in a backpack, pick up things a person drops, open and close doors, and help their owners get dressed or undressed. [6]Finally, "seizure alert/response" dogs are trained to respond to a person's seizures and either stay with the person, or go get help. [7]Some dogs are even trained to hit a button on a console to automatically dial 911. [8]When the dog hears the operator's voice over the speaker, the dog starts barking.

   A. Many dogs perform jobs for humans.

   B. Dogs help disabled people in a number of ways.

   C. "Hearing" dogs are similar to guide dogs.

   D. Some dogs are amazing.

___ 5. [1]In 1922, William Baerg, a scientist at the University of Arkansas, coaxed a black widow spider to bite him on the finger. [2]Baerg let the spider sink its fangs in for a full five seconds, then kept a diary of his reactions:

• [3]July 10, 8:25 AM: When spider removed, the pain keeps on growing, a sharp piercing sensation.
   [4]12:20 PM: Pain in hips rather severe. [5]Chest feels cramped; breathing and speech are fitful.
   [6]4:30: Nervous shaking, present since noon, is more noticeable now.
   [7]5:15: Arrived at the hospital.
• [8]July 11, 6:00 AM: Pain in legs and hips very severe.
• [9]July 12, 5:50 AM: Slept for short periods; much troubled by nightmares. [10]As soon as I fell asleep, I would dream that I was working with spiders.

[11]Altogether, Baerg spent three days in the hospital and needed a week to recover fully. [12]As proof that the spider was poisonous, he later wrote in a scientific journal, the results were "all that could be desired."

   A. William Baerg often carried out dangerous experiments for the sake of science.

   B. Being bitten by a black widow spider is not serious.

   C. Baerg would probably let another black widow spider bite him.

   D. Baerg became ill as a result of being bitten by the spider.

THE BASICS OF ARGUMENT: Test A

In each of the following groups, one statement is the point, and the other statements are support for the point. Identify each point with a **P** and each statement of support with an **S**.

Group 1

____ A. It is common for people to cry at weddings and funerals.

____ B. People tend to dress up for both weddings and funerals.

____ C. As strange as it may seem, weddings and funerals share certain characteristics.

____ D. Both weddings and funerals mark a passage from one state of being to another.

Group 2

____ A. Jumping spiders can leap up to fifty times their own body length.

____ B. Spitting spiders shoot streams of glue to capture their prey.

____ C. Although many people dislike them, spiders are capable of some amazing feats.

____ D. Orb weavers can spin silk as strong as steel and a thousand times as elastic.

Group 3

____ A. People who work from home don't have to dress for work.

____ B. For many people, working from home is a good thing.

____ C. Working from home eliminates the hassle of commuting to work.

____ D. Parents find that working at home enables them to better keep an eye on their children.

Group 4

____ A. In the early 1800s, medical doctors used dangerous methods to "heal" their patients.

____ B. Leeches were used to drain a person of what was believed to be "excess" blood.

____ C. Powerful chemical laxatives were used to "cleanse" the body of impurities.

____ D. Blistering ointments were applied to the skin in the belief that they would draw off impurities and thereby cure the patient.

Group 5

____ A. In Mary Shelley's *Frankenstein*, a scientist's creation becomes a killer.

____ B. Many science fiction stories deal with the theme of "mad" scientists.

____ C. In *The Strange Case of Dr. Jekyll and Mr. Hyde*, a mild-mannered doctor drinks a potion which frees his evil twin.

____ D. In *Jurassic Park,* scientists clone dinosaur DNA to create living dinosaurs which soon attack people.

Name: _____

Section_____ Date _____

SCORE: (Number correct) × 10 = _____%

THE BASICS OF ARGUMENT: Test B

A. (1–8). In each of the following groups, one statement is the point, and the other statements are support for the point. Identify each point with a **P** and each statement of support with an **S**.

Group 1

____ A. The telephone industry uses lasers to send phone calls under the ocean to Europe.

____ B. Automobile manufacturers use lasers for many purposes in making cars.

____ C. Surgeons use lasers to vaporize brain tumors.

____ D. Lasers harness the power of light for a wide range of uses.

Group 2

____ A. One piece of advice warned nobles not to blow their nose with the same hand that they used to hold their food.

____ B. Fifteenth- and sixteenth-century advice to nobles about manners can seem shockingly gross to modern readers.

____ C. Another piece of advice was that one should not blow his nose on the tablecloth.

____ D. Finally, fifteenth- and sixteenth-century nobles were advised not to spit on the table.

B. (9.) Below is a point followed by three items of information. Put a check (✓) next to the **one** item that logically supports the point.

Point: Advertising is a waste of time and money.

____ A. Advertising adds to the cost of products. People ignore most advertising because they know it paints an unrealistic picture of the products. It's very annoying to be watching a program on TV and have that program interrupted by commercials.

____ B. Advertising can help us to make decisions about products we might like to own. Some TV commercials are more entertaining than regular programming. Most people would not be aware of new products without advertising.

____ C. In America, advertising is everywhere. Ads appear on shopping carts, on video screens at sports stadiums, and atop parking meters. The average American is exposed to 500 ads a day. Advertising is a multi-billion dollar business.

(Continues on next page)

C. (10.) Read the three items of supporting evidence. Then put a check (✓) next to the point that is most logically supported by that evidence.

Support:

- The central Midwestern states have been called "tornado alley."
- Hurricanes usually occur along the southeastern and gulf coasts of the United States.
- Over the past one hundred years, earthquakes have repeatedly shaken California.

Point: Which of the following conclusions is best supported by all the evidence above?

_____ A. Violent weather is common in the Midwestern states.

_____ B. Natural disasters can occur in any part of the United States.

_____ C. The northeastern United States is free from natural disasters.

_____ D. Certain regions of the United States experience different kinds of natural disasters.

THE BASICS OF ARGUMENT: Test C

A. Each point is followed by three statements that provide logical support and two that do not. In the spaces, write the letters of the **three** logical statements of support.

1–3. *Point:* My uncle was very skilled at home improvements.

    A. He converted his garage into another bedroom.

    B. He made built-in bookcases for his den.

    C. He worked as an insurance salesman for forty years.

    D. His house was a row house with a small backyard.

    E. He refinished the kitchen cabinets.

Items that logically support the point: _____ _____ _____

4–6. *Point:* When it comes to new inventions and designs, the experts are sometimes wrong.

    A. Bill Gates founded Microsoft when he was in his early twenties.

    B. Automaker Henry Ford thought the Volkswagen Beetle would be a failure.

    C. In 1894, the president of the Royal Society, Lord Kelvin, predicted that radio had no future.

    D. Although television was invented before World War II, it didn't become widely available until after the war.

    E. In 1943, Thomas Watson, the chairman of IBM, forecast a world market for "maybe only five computers."

Items that logically support the point: _____ _____ _____

7–9. *Point:* Even though it's been outlawed in every country in the world, slavery is still a global problem.

    A. Women and girls have been kidnapped and forced to work as prostitutes in many countries throughout the world.

    B. In ancient Rome, a slave named Spartacus led an unsuccessful slave revolt.

    C. The United States outlawed slavery when Lincoln signed the Emancipation Proclamation in 1863.

    D. Modern-day slaves work as sugarcane cutters in Haiti and southern Pakistan.

    E. In Asia and Africa, children are sometimes sold into slavery to help pay off their parents' debts.

Items that logically support the point: _____ _____ _____

(Continues on next page)

B. (10.) Below is a point followed by three items of information. Put a check (✓) next to the **one** item that logically supports the point.

Point: When we were growing up, my dad was very strict.

____ A. He worked two jobs to support the family. He was often so tired that he would fall asleep in his chair. He rarely had time to see us when we participated in sports and in school plays. We had to be quiet when he slept during the day.

____ B. We were assigned certain chores, and if we didn't do them well, he withheld our allowance. We had to let him know where we were every hour of the day. He always made us do our homework before allowing us to watch TV.

____ C. When we were little, he read aloud to us. He coached us when we played soccer and baseball. He took us fishing and to sporting events. He often told us that we were the most important things in his life.

THE BASICS OF ARGUMENT: Test D

A. (1–8). In each of the following groups, one statement is the point, and the other statements are support for the point. Identify each point with a **P** and each statement of support with an **S**.

Group 1

____ A. Like young children, many elderly people need help while eating and undressing.

____ B. Just as a toddler cannot be left home alone, an older person suffering from Alzheimer's disease must be under constant watch.

____ C. Both the very old and the very young are likely to fall.

____ D. The very old and the very young are similar in some ways.

Group 2

____ A. Rubber factories boomed with the demand for tires.

____ B. New rolling mills had to be built to supply sheet steel for car bodies.

____ C. In the 1920s, the mass production of automobiles had a huge effect on the American economy.

____ D. Paint and glass suppliers had more business than ever before.

B. (9.) Below is a point followed by three items of information. Put a check (✓) next to the **one** item that logically supports the point.

Point: My neighbor is active in our community.

____ A. He grows vegetables in his backyard. He installed solar paneling on his roof. He drives a hybrid car that gets great gas mileage. He bought new energy-saving appliances.

____ B. He works for a large corporation. He travels often on business trips. He sends his kids to a private school. He drives a Lexus. When he walks his dog, he says hello to the people he sees.

____ C. He organized the neighborhood town watch. Before last month's local election, he passed out flyers urging people to vote for a certain candidate. He's on the school board and also a volunteer firefighter.

(Continues on next page)

C. (10.) Read the three items of supporting evidence. Then put a check (✓) next to the point that is most logically supported by that evidence.

Support:

- Two Englishmen dueled because their dogs had fought.
- Two Italians dueled because they disagreed over which of two poets was the more talented.
- One British nobleman killed a man in a duel after disagreeing about whose property had more wildlife to hunt.

Point: Which of the following conclusions is best supported by all the evidence above?

____ A. People often died during duels.

____ B. Some duels were fought for ridiculous reasons.

____ C. Dueling was never as popular in America as it was in Europe.

____ D. Dueling is no longer considered an acceptable way of solving disputes.

Name: _____

Section_____ Date_____

SCORE: (Number correct) × 12.5 = _____%

COMBINED SKILLS: Test A

After reading the passage, write the letter of the best answer to each question. (For your convenience, the passage is reprinted on the second page of the test.)

[1]In the popular imagination, Indian attacks were the most common reason for injury and death among settlers heading west in wagon trains. [2]The reality, however, was quite different. [3]Many settler diaries record examples of Indian bands assisting travelers with directions or trading food for manufactured goods. [4]It's true that instances of begging and horse theft did at times occur. [5]However, the notion of circled wagon trains under constant Indian attack is the result of Hollywood's imagination. [6]The wagons were, indeed, circled every night, but the people usually slept and cooked outside the ring while the animals were corralled inside. [7]Rather than Indians, by far the number-one threat that faced western settlers was disease, contributing to about 90 percent of fatalities. [8]Asiatic cholera, which broke out in 1849, 1850, and 1852, was the most fearsome killer, followed distantly by mountain fever and scurvy.

____ 1. The implied main idea of the passage is best expressed in which of the following sentences?

    A. Disease, not Indian attacks, was the major cause of death among settlers heading west.

    B. Hollywood was largely responsible for spreading myths about Indian attacks on settlers.

    C. Settlers circled their wagons every night not to protect themselves but to corral their animals.

    D. Diseases killed a large number of western settlers in the 1840s and 1850s.

____ 2. Indian bands sometimes

    A. assisted settlers with directions.

    B. traded food to settlers in exchange for manufactured goods.

    C. begged and stole from settlers.

    D. did all of the above.

____ 3. Disease contributed to what percentage of fatalities among settlers?

    A. 10 percent.

    B. 70 percent.

    C. 90 percent.

    D. 95 percent.

____ 4. The relationship of sentence 2 to sentence 1 is one of

    A. time.

    B. addition.

    C. cause and effect.

    D. contrast.

(Continues on next page)

[1]In the popular imagination, Indian attacks were the most common reason for injury and death among settlers heading west in wagon trains. [2]The reality, however, was quite different. [3]Many settler diaries record examples of Indian bands assisting travelers with directions or trading food for manufactured goods. [4]It's true that instances of begging and horse theft did at times occur. [5]However, the notion of circled wagon trains under constant Indian attack is the result of Hollywood's imagination. [6]The wagons were, indeed, circled every night, but the people usually slept and cooked outside the ring while the animals were corralled inside. [7]Rather than Indians, by far the number-threat that faced western settlers was disease, contributing to about 90 percent of fatalities. [8]Asiatic cholera, which broke out in 1849, 1850, and 1852, was the most fearsome killer, followed distantly by mountain fever and scurvy.

____ 5. In sentence 5, the word which signals a cause and effect relationship is

    A. *however.*

    B. *under.*

    C. *constant.*

    D. *result.*

____ 6. This passage suggests that

    A. settlers heading west had no way to cure outbreaks of diseases like Asiatic cholera and mountain fever.

    B. all Indians were enemies of the settlers.

    C. it was not dangerous to travel across the United States in the middle of the 1800s.

    D. all of the above.

____ 7. We can conclude that Hollywood promoted the idea that settlers were under constant Indian attack because

    A. Indian attacks were more entertaining to watch than people dying of disease.

    B. most Hollywood movie makers disliked Indians.

    C. Hollywood movie producers had read the diaries of western settlers.

    D. some Hollywood movie producers had themselves been western settlers.

____ 8. Write the letter of the statement that is the point of the following argument. The other statements are support for that point.

    A. Sometimes Indians helped settlers.

    B. Few settlers died from Indian attacks.

    C. Settlers did not put their wagons in a circle to protect against Indian attack.

    D. The popular view of western settlers and Indians is unrealistic.

COMBINED SKILLS: Test B

After reading the passage, write the letter of the best answer to each question. (For your convenience, the passage is reprinted on the second page of the test.)

> [1]After forty years of separation from his identical twin, James Lewis began his search for his long-lost brother. [2]They had been separated a few weeks after birth and were adopted by different families. [3]Their reunion took place at the home of the other twin—James Springer. [4]Upon meeting, they found that they were comparable in ways other than their first names. [5]Both had married a woman named Betty, been divorced, and remarried a woman named Sally. [6]Both had had similar jobs as deputy sheriffs, McDonald's employees, and gas station attendants. [7]Both liked to build wood furniture in their basement workshops. [8]Both put on 10 pounds as teenagers and lost it later. [9]Both had the same favorite subjects in school, were bad spellers, and suffered from bad headaches and sleeping problems. [10]All in all, they shared 27 matching characteristics.

____ 1. In sentence 4, the word *comparable* means

   A. fortunate.
   B. different.
   C. similar.
   D. separate.

____ 2. Which of the following best expresses the main idea of the paragraph?

   A. Identical twins named James were reunited after forty years of separation.
   B. Identical twins found that they had similar jobs, wives with the same first name, and similar interests.
   C. Upon meeting, identical twins found that they had a great deal in common.
   D. Upon meeting, identical twins found that they were truly identical in all respects.

____ 3. James Lewis and James Springer were separated

   A. all of their lives.
   B. a few weeks after birth.
   C. for only a few years.
   D. a few hours after they were born.

____ 4. James Lewis and James Springer were reunited

   A. at the home of a close friend of James Lewis.
   B. at the home of James Lewis.
   C. at the place where James Springer worked.
   D. at the home of James Springer.

(Continues on next page)

[1]After forty years of separation from his identical twin, James Lewis began his search for his long-lost brother. [2]They had been separated a few weeks after birth and were adopted by different families. [3]Their reunion took place at the home of the other twin—James Springer. [4]Upon meeting, they found that they were comparable in ways other than their first names. [5]Both had married a woman named Betty, been divorced, and remarried a woman named Sally. [6]Both had had similar jobs as deputy sheriffs, McDonald's employees, and gas station attendants. [7]Both liked to build wood furniture in their basement workshops. [8]Both put on 10 pounds as teenagers and lost it later. [9]Both had the same favorite subjects in school, were bad spellers, and suffered from bad headaches and sleeping problems. [10]All in all, they shared 27 matching characteristics.

_____ 5. The first word of the first sentence and the last word of sentence 8 signal a relationship of

    A. time.

    B. addition.

    C. contrast.

    D. cause and effect.

_____ 6. This passage suggests that

    A. because James Lewis and James Springer had been raised by different parents, they were different in a number of ways.

    B. the similarities between identical twins can be amazing.

    C. James Lewis and James Springer are not like most other identical twins.

    D. James Springer was never curious about his long-lost brother.

_____ 7. We can conclude from this passage that

    A. both James Lewis and James Springer were deeply unhappy about having been adopted.

    B. some personal characteristics are not influenced by how a person is raised.

    C. most adopted children never learn who their birth parents were.

    D. James Lewis and James Springer will begin to dislike each other after they get to know one another.

8. Label the point of the following argument with a P and the two statements of support with an S. Label with an X the statement that is neither the point nor the support of the argument.

    _____ A. James Springer and James Lewis both liked to build wood furniture.

    _____ B. James Springer and James Lewis had the same favorite subjects in school.

    _____ C. James Springer and James Lewis both suffered from bad headaches and sleeping problems.

    _____ D. James Springer and James Lewis had similar interests and abilities.

COMBINED SKILLS: Test C

After reading the passage, write the letter of the best answer to each question. (For your convenience, the passage is reprinted on the second page of the test.)

[1]In today's fast-paced world, people often try to persuade us to buy one thing or another. [2]How can you reduce the chance that you'll be pressured into making a decision that is not in your best interest? [3]One way is to sleep on it. [4]The persuader may respond to your sleep-on-it suggestion by saying, "This offer is good for today only." [5]Chances are that's a sign he or she is afraid you will come to realize the offer is not as good as it seems. [6]Another way to avoid buying something that you'll later regret is to list all of the reasons why you should not buy the product. [7]Arguing against the decision will help activate your critical thinking skills. [8]It's also helpful to discuss important decisions with a friend, who might be able to point out disadvantages that you have overlooked. [9]Finally, learn to trust your gut feelings when something doesn't feel quite right. [10]If you feel that you're being psychologically pressured or cornered, you probably are. [11]As a general rule, if you feel any sense of doubt, play it safe and do nothing.

____ 1. In sentence 7, the word *activate* means
    A. turn on.
    B. distract from.
    C. turn off.
    D. reduce.

____ 2. Which of the following best expresses the main idea of the paragraph?
    A. In today's world, people often pressure us to make bad decisions.
    B. There are several ways to avoid making decisions that are not in your best interest.
    C. If you feel that you're being psychologically pressured or cornered, you probably are.
    D. If you sleep on an offer, you may come to realize that the offer was not as good as it first seemed.

____ 3. A general rule of decision-making is to
    A. sleep on it.
    B. discuss important decisions with a friend.
    C. do nothing if you feel any sense of doubt.
    D. list all the reasons you should not buy a product.

____ 4. If a persuader suggests that an offer is good for today only, that's a sign that
    A. he or she is afraid you will come to realize the offer is not as good as it seems.
    B. the offer is a good one, and you should immediately take advantage of it.
    C. the persuader is totally dishonest.
    D. you should discuss the decision with a friend.

(Continues on next page)

[1]In today's fast-paced world, people often try to persuade us to buy one thing or another. [2]How can you reduce the chance that you'll be pressured into making a decision that is not in your best interest? [3]One way is to sleep on it. [4]The persuader may respond to your sleep-on-it suggestion by saying, "This offer is good for today only." [5]Chances are that's a sign he or she is afraid you will come to realize the offer is not as good as it seems. [6]Another way to avoid buying something that you'll later regret is to list all of the reasons why you should not buy the product. [7]Arguing against the decision will help activate your critical thinking skills. [8]It's also helpful to discuss important decisions with a friend, who might be able to point out disadvantages that you have overlooked. [9]Finally, learn to trust your gut feelings when something doesn't feel quite right. [10]If you feel that you're being psychologically pressured or cornered, you probably are. [11]As a general rule, if you feel any sense of doubt, play it safe and do nothing.

_____ 5. The relationship of sentence 6 to sentence 5 is one of

    A. time.

    B. addition.

    C. contrast.

    D. cause and effect.

_____ 6. This passage suggests that

    A. most of the decisions people make are wise ones.

    B. people are often pressured into making decisions that are not in their best interest.

    C. it's often better to accept an offer than to turn it down.

    D. our gut feelings are often wrong.

_____ 7. We can conclude that the author of this passage

    A. has little experience dealing with high-pressure situations.

    B. was himself a high-pressure salesman.

    C. knows something about psychology.

    D. was pressured into making many poor decisions.

8. In the following group, one statement is the point, and the other statements are support for the point. Write the letter of the statement that is the point of the argument.

    _____ A. It's a good idea to list all the reasons why you should not buy the product.

    _____ B. One way to react to an offer is to sleep on it.

    _____ C. There are several ways to avoid being pressured into making bad decisions.

    _____ D. Discuss the offer with a friend, who might be able to point out disadvantages that you have overlooked.

COMBINED SKILLS: Test D

After reading the passage, write the letter of the best answer to each question. (For your convenience, the passage is reprinted on the second page of the test.)

[1]December is not only the joyous season; it's the mating season as well. [2]According to birth records in the U.S. and many other countries, the last month of the year has the highest number of conceptions that result in births. [3]Researchers at the University of Michigan tracked the peaks and dips in U.S. birth rates for a thirty-year period. [4]They found that the peak season for births is September, nine months from the frosty days of December. [5]On the other hand, they found that there's a lull in births during April and May. [6]This lack of activity suggests that the hot nights of July and August may actually cool people's romantic passions. [7]While the weather may account for some of the variations in birth rates, the researchers also suggest that the holiday celebrations in December may play a part in holiday conceptions. [8]"People are spending time with their family, seeing nieces and nephews and thinking about how wonderful kids are," says researcher Jeffrey Miron. [9]He believes that "many of these conceptions may be due, in part, to a 'warm family effect.'"

____ 1. In sentence 5, the word *lull* means

    A. increase.

    B. decrease.

    C. absence.

    D. peak.

____ 2. The main idea of the paragraph is expressed in its

    A. first sentence.

    B. third sentence.

    C. next-to-last sentence.

    D. last sentence.

____ 3. The peak season for births is

    A. July and August.

    B. December.

    C. September.

    D. around the holidays.

____ 4. The relationship of sentence 5 to sentence 4 is one of

    A. addition.

    B. cause and effect.

    C. contrast.

    D. time.

(Continues on next page)

[1]December is not only the joyous season; it's the mating season as well. [2]According to birth records in the U.S. and many other countries, the last month of the year has the highest number of conceptions that result in births. [3]Researchers at the University of Michigan tracked the peaks and dips in U.S. birth rates for a thirty-year period. [4]They found that the peak season for births is September, nine months from the frosty days of December. [5]On the other hand, they found that there's a lull in births during April and May. [6]This lack of activity suggests that the hot nights of July and August may actually cool people's romantic passions. [7]While the weather may account for some of the variations in birth rates, the researchers also suggest that the holiday celebrations in December may play a part in holiday conceptions. [8]"People are spending time with their family, seeing nieces and nephews and thinking about how wonderful kids are," says researcher Jeffrey Miron. [9]He believes that "many of these conceptions may be due, in part, to a 'warm family effect.'"

____ 5. Sentence 9 expresses a relationship of
    A. contrast.
    B. cause and effect.
    C. addition.
    D. time.

____ 6. This passage suggests that
    A. holiday celebrations in December encourage couples to have children.
    B. not everyone celebrates December holidays.
    C. the high number of conceptions in December is entirely due to cold weather.
    D. holiday celebrations have become bothersome for many people.

____ 7. We can infer from this passage that
    A. people don't like to mate on hot, sticky nights.
    B. the weather has little to do with conception rates,
    C. most American couples use birth control.
    D. hot-climate countries have lower birth rates than cool-climate countries.

8. Label the point of the following argument with a P and the two statements of support with an S. Label with an X the statement that is neither the point nor the support of the argument.
    ____ A. The conception rate is highest during the frosty month of December.
    ____ B. Holiday celebrations seem to play a part in the high rate of December conceptions.
    ____ C. Fewer children are conceived during the hot nights of July and August.
    ____ D. The weather plays a part in conception rates.

ANSWERS TO THE TESTS IN THE TEST BANK

CONSONANTS: Test A

1. gravy
2. corner
3. gentle
4. science
5. center
6. B
7. A
8. D
9. C
10. D

CONSONANTS: Test B

1. C
2. B
3. D
4. A
5. C
6. scratch
7. unclean
8. sand
9. retrain
10. playground

CONSONANTS: Test C

1. cards
2. garden
3. grade school
4. spring
5. traces
6. checkers
7. thin
8. chipped
9. knife
10. writer

CONSONANTS: Test D

1. hunt
2. surprised
3. inspect
4. Philadelphia
5. shower
6. thirty
7. rough
8. most excellent
9. picked
10. well-known

VOWELS: Test A

1. $\bar{e}$
2. $\bar{a}$
3. r
4. $\breve{o}$
5. $\bar{\imath}$
6. $\breve{\imath}$
7. $\breve{a}$
8. silent
9. r
10. $\breve{\imath}$
11. $\breve{a}$
12. r
13. $\bar{o}$
14. r
15. $\bar{a}$
16. trace
17. mine
18. team
18. float
20. go

VOWELS: Test B

1. rag
2. flame
3. set
4. clean
5. fill
6. bite
7. block
8. slope
9. punch
10. mute
11. lime
12. shame
13. braid
14. load
15. ago
16. long
17. short
18. short
19. short
20. long

VOWELS: Test C

1. apple
2. blocks
3. jet
4. hike
5. A
6. breed
7. B
8. C
9. A
10. B

VOWELS: Test D

1. A
2. C
3. C
4. A
5. A
6. B
7. B
8. A
9. A
10. B

SYLLABLES: Test A

1. con-test, 1
2. pa-per, 2
3. wa-ter, 2
4. win-ner, 1
5. ex-cuse, 1
6. guess-work, 5
7. jun-gle, 3
8. dis-like, 4
9. mid-dle, 3
10. soft-ness, 4

SYLLABLES: Test B

1. re-fer-ral, 2, 1
2. sup-port-ing, 1, 4
3. hor-ri-ble, 1, 3
4. dis-con-nect, 4, 1
5. for-mal-ly, 1, 4
6. jel-ly-fish, 1, 5
7. in-no-cent, 1, 2
8. ice-break-er, 5, 4
9. suc-cess-ful, 1, 4
10. la-dy-like, 2, 5

SYLLABLES: Test C

1. vam-pire	6. con-certs
2. E-ven	7. Po-land
3. ca-ble	8. mum-ble
4. in-cur-a-ble	9. re-new-ing
5. eye-sore	10. hand-cuffs

SYLLABLES: Test D

1. af-ter	6. ar-ranged	9. pre-scrip-tion
2. re-ports	7. a-way	10. through-out
3. peo-ple	8. a-ble	
4. re-u-nit-ing		
5. Fire-storm *or* Hot-line *or* Oak-land		

WORD PARTS: Test A

1. remove	6. forceful
2. supervisor	7. sheepish
3. elderly	8. previewing
4. misbehaved	9. manager
5. plumber	10. invention

WORD PARTS: Test B

1. telemarketer	6. lovely
2. postwar	7. punishment
3. audition	8. autopilot
4. inflatable	9. conservationist
5. inspection	10. preserve

WORD PARTS: Test C

1. relocate	6. unlikely
2. monologue	7. transported
3. indistinct	8. astonishment
4. biological	9. inseparable
5. benefit	10. motherless

WORD PARTS: Test D

1. pedometer	6. therapist
2. audible	7. stressful
3. subdivided	8. misleading
4. expired	9. undecided
5. fundamentalism	10. Prevention

GETTING STARTED : Test

1. C	5. C	9. D
2. D	6. B	10. A
3. D	7. B	
4. B	8. D	

DICTIONARY USE: Test A

1. bronze	11. piece
2. brother	12. reveal
3. crystal	13. tragedy
4. cucumber	14. invention
5. headlight	15. disappear
6. haze	16. equipment
7. rocky	17. hi
8. rodeo	18. sit
9. whitefish	19. go
10. whisper	20. hat

DICTIONARY USE: Test B

1. sus•pect sə-spĕkt′ *or* sŭs′pĕkt′		
2. giv•en gĭv′ən	11. leaves	
3. most•ly mōst′lē	12. heroes	
4. arm•chair ärm′châr′	13. gypsies	
5. brain•storm brān′stôrm′	14. cacti *or* cactuses	
6. wash•bowl wŏsh′bōl′ *or* wôsh′bōl′		
7. n., v., adj.	15. hammerhead	19. iota
8. adj., adv., v.	16. sting	20. sting
9. v., n., adj.	17. hammerhead, iota	
10. pron., adj.	18. bluebird, hammerhead	

DICTIONARY USE: Test C

1. coaster	11. heavy
2. coachman	12. gin rummy
3. gull	13. official
4. guilt	14. awful
5. muzzle	15. total
6. myrtle	16. cashier
7. C	17. ten
8. C	18. go
9. B	19. sit
10. A	20. ago

DICTIONARY USE: Test D

1. bev•er•age bĕv′ər-ĭj, bĕv′rĭj	11. sentries
2. eight•i•eth ā′tē-ĭth	12. broke, broken, (breaking)
3. poi•son poi′zən	
4. man•han•dle măn′hăn′dəl	13. B
5. sym•pho•ny sĭm′fə-nē	14. D
6. n., v., prep.	15. B
7. n., v.	16. overblown, pillow
8. n., adj., v.	17. progressive, pillow
9. more, most	18. decorate, progressive, overblown
10. swam, swum, (swimming)	19. decorate, overblown
	20. pillow

VOCABULARY IN CONTEXT: Test A

1. a bright red dress, a rose in her hair, a big hat; C
2. shouted insults at him, threatened his life; B
3. part 6. C 9. B
4. remember 7. A 10. A
5. deep 8. B

VOCABULARY IN CONTEXT: Test B

1. B 6. C
2. A 7. B
3. B 8. B
4. C 9. C
5. B 10. A

VOCABULARY IN CONTEXT: Test C

1. B 6. B
2. C 7. A
3. B 8. B
4. B 9. B
5. C 10. A

VOCABULARY IN CONTEXT: Test D

1. B 6. B
2. C 7. A
3. C 8. B
4. A 9. B
5. B 10. A

MAIN IDEAS: Test A

1. relative
2. shape
3. compliment
4. award
5. clues

Answers will vary:
6-7. lunch, dinner
8-9. poodle, boxer

10-11. Labor Day, Easter
12-13. stove, freezer
14-15. silver, bronze
Answers to second items will vary:
16-17. music; jazz
18-19. athlete; Venus Williams
20-21. wild animal; bear
22-23. coin; penny
24-25. snack; raisins

MAIN IDEAS: Test B

1. vehicle
2. leisure activity
3. musical instrument
4. science
5. fish

Answers will vary:
6-7. "yes," "maybe"
8-9. fruit salad, chocolate cake
10-11. house painting, road repair
12-13. algebra, Spanish

Answers to second items will vary:
14-15. farm animal; cow
16-17. organ; lungs
18-19. drink; iced tea
20. B

MAIN IDEAS: Test C

1. B
2. C
3. C
4. B
5. B

MAIN IDEAS: Test D

1. B 6. B
2. B 7. B
3. B 8. A
4. A 9. A
5. B 10. C

SUPPORTING DETAILS: Test A

A.

Group 1	Group 2
A. MI	A. SD
B. SD	B. MI
C. SD	C. SD

B. • Special Checking
  • Money Market
    Checking
9. Next
10. Finally

SUPPORTING DETAILS: Test B

(Wording of outline and map answers may vary.)

A. . . . can have
   undesired effects.
2. Aggression
3. Child abuse
4. C
5. third

B. . . . product life cycle.
7. Growth stage
8. Maturity stage
9. Decline stage: Sales
   and profits slip and
   eventually fade away
10. B

SUPPORTING DETAILS: Test C

1. B   6. C
2. B   7. B
3. A   8. Finally
4. C   9. To substitute for verbal messages
5. C   10. To accent what we are saying

(Wording of outline answers in Supporting Details Tests C and D may vary.)

SUPPORTING DETAILS: Test D

A. 1. For pleasure or enjoyment
    2. To provide emotional support for the speaker
    3. To understand the message of a speaker
    4. To accept or reject a message
    5. One, second, Another, Finally
B. 6. To entertain others
    7. To help people remember something important
    8. To help people overcome addictions or fears
    9. To begin with
   10. last

FINDING MAIN IDEAS: Test A

1. 1   4. 9
2. 2   5. 1
3. 2

FINDING MAIN IDEAS: Test B

1. 1   4. 1
2. 2   5. 8
3. 2

FINDING MAIN IDEAS: Test C

1. 1   4. 2
2. 2   5. 2
3. 6

FINDING MAIN IDEAS: Test D

1. 2   4. 1
2. 1   5. 8
3. 2

SIGNAL WORDS I: Test A

1. A; also   6. During
2. E; then   7. while
3. C; During   8. Afterward
4. D; In addition 9. When
5. B; As   10. B

SIGNAL WORDS I: Test B

1. D; In addition 6. One
2. A; another   7. Then
3. B; During   8. later
4. C; First of all 9. Another
5. E; One   10. Moreover

SIGNAL WORDS I: Test C

1. One   6. Finally
2. Another   7. When
3. third   8. After
4. Then (or Next) 9. later
5. Next (or Then) 10. B

SIGNAL WORDS I: Test D

1. during   6. The power to reward
2. While   7. The ability to punish
3. later   8. Organizational power
4. B   9. Expert power
5. A   10. Personality power

SIGNAL WORDS II: Test A

1. A; however*   6. reason
2. E; such as   7. causes
3. B; On the other hand* 8. leads to
4. D; Since   9. For example
5. C; result   10. instance

Answers for items 1 and 3 may be interchanged.

SIGNAL WORDS II: Test B

1. D; For example   6. While
2. B; Because   7. On the other hand
3. C; Despite   8. different
4. E; including   9. In contrast
5. A; As a result 10. A

SIGNAL WORDS II: Test C

1. Therefore
2. since
3. result
4. B
5. different
6. while
7. C

8–10. *(Wording of answers may vary.)*
1. More workers are in service industries where they must deal with difficult customers.
2. The economy is unpredictable, causing workers to fear they might lose their jobs.
3. Rapid changes in computer technology force workers to develop new skills quickly or be laid off.

SIGNAL WORDS II: Test D

1. different
2. On the other hand
3. rather than
4. instead
5. affect
6. due to
7. led
8. Secondly
9. Finally
10. cause

INFERENCES: Test A

1–2. A, C
3–8. B, D
G, H
I, J
9–10. A, D

INFERENCES: Test B

1–3. B, C, F
4–7. B, C
E, G
8–10. B, D, F

INFERENCES: Test C

1–3. A, B, D
4–7. B, C
F, H
8–10. A, D, F

INFERENCES: Test D

1. C
2. D
3. B
4. B
5. D

ARGUMENT: Test A

Group 1	Group 2
A. S	A. S
B. S	B. S
C. P	C. P
D. S	D. S

Group 3	Group 4
A. S	A. P
B. P	B. S
C. S	C. S
D. S	D. S

Group 5
A. S
B. P
C. S
D. S

ARGUMENT: Test B

A. (1–8.) Group 1	Group 2
A. S	A. S
B. S	B. P
C. S	C. S
D. P	D. S

B. 9. A
C. 10. D

ARGUMENT : Test C

A. 1–3. A, B, E
   4–6. B, C, E
   7–9. A, D, E
B. 10. B

ARGUMENT: Test D

A. (1–8.) *Group 1*   *Group 2*
       A. S   A. S
       B. S   B. S
       C. S   C. P
       D. P   D. S

B. 9. C
C. 10. B

COMBINED SKILLS: Test A

1. A   5. D
2. D   6. A
3. C   7. A
4. D   8. D

COMBINED SKILLS: Test B

1. C   5. A
2. C   6. B
3. B   7. B
4. D   8. A. S
            B. S
            C. X
            D. P

COMBINED SKILLS: Test C

1. A   5. B
2. B   6. B
3. C   7. C
4. A   8. A. S
            B. S
            C. P
            D. S

COMBINED SKILLS: Test D

1. B   5. B
2. A   6. A
3. C   7. A
4. C   8. A. S
            B. X
            C. S
            D. P